VARSITY GREEN

Varsity Green

A BEHIND THE SCENES LOOK AT CULTURE AND CORRUPTION IN COLLEGE ATHLETICS

Mark Yost

STANFORD ECONOMICS AND FINANCE

An Imprint of Stanford University Press

Stanford, California 2010

Stanford University Press
Stanford, California

Library of Congress Cataloging-in-Publication Data

Yost, Mark.
  Varsity green : a behind the scenes look at culture and corruption in
college athletics / Mark Yost.
      p. cm.
  Includes bibliographical references and index.
  ISBN 978-0-8047-6969-3 (cloth : alk. paper)
    1. College sports—Economic aspects—United States. 2. College
sports—Corrupt practices—United States. I. Title.
GV351.Y67 2010
796.04'30973—dc22

                                                            2009022487

Printed in the United States of America on acid-free, archival-
quality paper

Typeset at Stanford University Press in Helvetica and 10.5/15 Minion

Special discounts for bulk quantities of Stanford Economics and
Finance are available to corporations, professional associations, and
other organizations. For details and discount information, contact the
special sales department of Stanford University Press. Tel: (650) 736-
1783, Fax: (650) 736-1784

To George
With All My Love
Dad

CONTENTS

Introduction: The Huggins Factor   1

1   The Entertainment Product   13

2   An Inauspicious Beginning   31

3   Who's Really the BCS Champion?   48

4   Money Madness   64

5   Mud Rooms and Electron Microscopes   79

6   How Much Does That Stadium Really Cost?   97

7   Coaches Cash In, Too   115

8   A Boost Up   131

9   Breakin' All the Rules   147

10   The NCAA: Cartel or Mafia?   159

11   The Kids   174

Epilogue   189

References   197

INTRODUCTION:
THE HUGGINS FACTOR

In March 2006, Kansas State University, which is known more for academics than athletics, shocked the college basketball world by hiring coach Bob Huggins. It was, arguably, the oddest marriage in the history of college sports.

Huggins, fifty-two, had compiled a record of 567-199 (.740) over twenty-four seasons. He'd spent the past eighteen years at the University of Cincinnati, where he built a nationally ranked college basketball program that distinguished itself both on the court and as one of Nike's best-selling collegiate brands. He was ranked eighth in winning percentage and total victories among active Division I head coaches. Huggins's teams had gone on to postseason play in twenty-one of his twenty-four seasons, including fifteen NCAA Tournament appearances. His string of fourteen consecutive trips to the NCAA Tournament ranked as the third-longest streak among active coaches. Under Huggins, Cincinnati had won twenty or more games in all but four seasons; in two seasons they won thirty games, bringing his average to 23.5 victories per season.

In addition to one of the most impressive winning records in college basketball, Bob Huggins also brought a lot of baggage to tiny Manhattan, Kansas. He had been run out of town by University of Cincinnati president Nancy Zimpher, who finally had the guts to say "enough" to the popular but controversial coach. In her mind, Huggins's winning percentage and national stature no longer outweighed his outlandish personal behavior and his penchant for recruiting street thugs who had no place at a respectable university. In fact, in his last few years at the helm, his players had an appalling 0 percent graduation rate. Huggins could often be as brutish as his players, and an off-campus DWI conviction didn't help his image with the Cincinnati beat writers, who had found him increasingly difficult to cover.

It's these last few facts that make this whole story so bizarre. Yes, disgraced coaches such as Huggins have been fired before, only to be rehired by another school claiming that the coach in question had "changed" or "learned his lesson." But these disgraced coaches had never resurrected their careers at places like Kansas State, where President Jon Wefald had a well-known—and well-deserved—reputation as someone who not only understood the importance of balancing athletics and academics but had made it the hallmark of his thirty-year career. In fact, there is a book, *A University Renaissance*, about how he had done just that at Kansas State.

Before Bob Huggins showed up on campus, Kansas State was more often associated with *Fortune* and *Forbes* than the Final Four. It consistently ranked near the top of the Big 12 Conference in Graduation Success Rate, the NCAA's six-year rolling average of student-athlete academic success. It also did well in the NCAA's new Academic Progress Rate, a more real-time measure of an athletic department's success at getting students to hit the books as well as the blocking dummies and their jump shots. Historically, K-State has been one of the leading public institutions in producing Marshall, Truman, and Rhodes scholars. In short, Kansas State was no Kentucky or Memphis, where basketball ranks first ahead of everything else, and bio lab is a distant third or fourth on the college president's list of top priorities. Picking Bob Huggins as its new basketball coach seemed to go completely against everything for which K-State stood.

But on November 22, 2007, Kansas State proved the skeptics wrong. They showed that coaches such as Bob Huggins were sometimes a gamble worth taking. That's the day that the K-State men's basketball team played in the Old Spice Classic in Orlando, Florida, its first nationally televised, elite, preseason tournament appearance in decades. A few weeks later, the team made its first-ever appearance in the Jimmy V Basketball Classic at Madison Square Garden in New York City. Going into the 2007–8 season, K-State had what was arguably one of the best recruiting classes in the country, and for the first time in decades the basketball team was ranked in the Top 25 in the preseason college basketball polls. And it was all because they'd hired Bob Huggins.

But by the time the 2007 season rolled around, Huggins was long gone. Like many of the players he'd recruited, he left Kansas State after just one year. Yet it's fair to say that in that one season, Bob Huggins had a huge impact on Kansas State. And whether you see him as a pariah or a prodigy, there's no arguing that Bob Huggins resurrected a program that had long been dormant.

K-State hadn't won a conference title since 1977, hadn't been to the NCAA tourney since 1996, and had missed the postseason entirely since 1999. The year before Huggins showed up, K-State's basketball team posted a record of 15-13. In just one year under the controversial coach they improved to 22-11, vied for the Big 12 championship against archrival Kansas, and, many argue, should have received an invitation to the first round of the NCAA Tournament.

Huggins wasn't gone because he fell back into his old ways. He hadn't been caught on camera hitting a player, he hadn't recruited players with felony records, or racked up another DWI. No, on April 7, 2007, Bob Huggins's rehabilitation—at least in the eyes of the college sports world—was complete. That's the day he accepted the head-coaching job at West Virginia University, his alma mater and a perennial college basketball powerhouse. He was back on top, a little more than a year after having been sent packing in disgrace from Cincinnati. Huggins signed a five-year contract with West Virginia that paid him $800,000 in his first year, the same salary he was making at Kansas State.

Huggins didn't leave K-State in the lurch. He left his former assistant, Frank Martin, with an outstanding recruiting class, including Michael Beasley, the McDonald's All-American forward from Gaithersburg, Maryland. Not coincidentally, Beasley, like Huggins, spent just one year at K-State. In 2008, he was selected second overall in the NBA draft.

Beasley is a story in and of himself. Moreover, he's indicative of the culture—and conflict—in today's high-profile world of college basketball. His high school career spanned six different schools in five states. His last stop was Notre Dame Prep in Fitchburg, Massachusetts, one of the controversial "prep schools" where highly recruited athletes go to make sure that their grades are good enough to get them into whichever school offers them the best deal. By most evidence, such schools are nothing more than diploma mills, where players are guaranteed A's and B's for spending more time on the practice court than in the classroom.

The irony of this ongoing subterfuge in which players and schools play cat-and-mouse with NCAA academic eligibility rules is that most players of Beasley's caliber stay in college only for the NBA-mandatory one-year minimum. For the Michael Beasleys of the world, college is just a way station on the way to their final destination: the NBA. College is like the bogus high schools they attended, the elite summer basketball camps where they were scouted, and the all-star high school tournaments where they show off their skills. In short, college for most of these elite players is a means to an end. Nothing more.

So in some ways, Michael Beasley was as big a threat to Kansas State's reputation for academic excellence as Bob Huggins. He was in Manhattan, Kansas, for one thing and one thing only: to play basketball.

Frank Martin, Huggins's long-time assistant who took over the program, came with his own baggage. One of the outstanding coaches in the history of Florida high school basketball, he was later stripped of his titles—including an unprecedented undefeated season—when it was learned that his school had doctored transcripts to recruit players from outside the school district, a violation of state high school athletic association rules. Miami High was fined $2,500 and forced to reimburse the Florida High School Athletic Association more than $5,000 in expenses related to the investigation. Five of Martin's players, including Udonis Haslem, were barred from ever playing for Miami High again. Martin's explanation to me when I asked him about the scandal was an incredulous "That had nothing to do with me. That was all done in the transfer office."

Others saw it differently. Florida High School Athletic Association commissioner Ron Davis said in a statement: "This is one of the most, if not *the* most, blatant violations of FHSAA rules against recruiting that I have encountered in my seven years as commissioner of this association."

Of course, none of this stopped Kansas State from hiring Martin. Neither did it stop the University of Florida from recruiting Haslem, who, as a "leisure service management" major, became one of the key players who helped a young Billy Donovan put Gainesville on the college basketball map. Having helped cement the school's reputation as an up-and-coming college basketball powerhouse, Haslem did what most every other marquee college player does: he left school without a degree. And, like many other athletes who have outlasted their usefulness, he left without much of a future.

When Haslem left the University of Florida in 2002, he weighed more than three hundred pounds and had no prospects for an NBA career. This is how most college athletes end up. Interestingly, ESPN, *Sports Illustrated,* and the daily beat writers who cover these kids don't spend much time on these stories. Instead, they fuel the frenzy of college athletics by profiling the superstars, the less than 2 percent of college athletes who make it to the pros. In doing so, they're as complicit in the creation of today's corrupt college sports culture as the scouts, coaches, and academic advisers who lie to the hundreds of thousands of kids who will never make it to the pros.

Over time, Haslem slimmed down. He lost seventy pounds and played basketball in France for *ES Chalon-sur-Saone* in 2002–3, averaging 16.1 points and 9.4 rebounds per game. That was enough to get him a spot in the NBA Summer League and attract the attention of Miami Heat coach Pat Riley. On April 22, 2006, in a first-round playoff game against the Chicago Bulls, Haslem was ejected for throwing his mouthpiece at the referee.

All of this, of course, raises the question, Why in the world would Kansas State president Jon Wefald risk his school's academic reputation and hire Bob Huggins and Frank Martin? The short answer, as with everything in college athletics today, is "money." And it's not chump change.

Kansas State signed Bob Huggins to a five-year deal that would have paid him more than $1 million a year in base salary, shoe contracts, radio and TV money, and incentives. And they were more than willing to do it because coaches such as Huggins do more than resurrect athletic programs. They breathe life into a school's brand and marketing power. Huggins certainly did that for K-State.

"Bob Huggins gave us a national presence, both as a basketball team and as a university," said Bob Cavello, K-State's athletic director for business development. "It was something we'd never experienced."

"We wanted to find somebody that was going to take our program to the level all of us expect it to be," said Athletic Director Tim Weiser. "He started to feel like this was a place he could resume his career and do so in a successful way."

It paid off. To this day, K-State is still counting the cash that was generated from Huggins's brief tenure as the school's head basketball coach. Along with Huggins came a $10 million, all-school shoe and apparel contract with Nike to outfit all of K-State's varsity sports athletes. K-State, which has an annual athletic budget of $38 million, had been wooing Nike for a dozen years with no success. Weeks after Huggins showed up, Nike was the one that came calling.

With the arrival of Huggins, K-State also saw its school apparel go from a small regional brand to national prominence. Huggins's presence increased sales more than 30 percent and moved K-State into the top thirty-five in sales for College Licensing Corp., the company that handles apparel sales and merchandising for many colleges and universities.

"Before, we didn't sell much outside of our core Midwest market," Cavello said. "Now, you go to New York and California and see kids wearing K-State apparel. That's because Bob Huggins is, himself, a national brand. And in many ways he made us a national brand, too."

Huggins had similar success during his sixteen winning seasons at Cincinnati. He helped develop the now-familiar school logo that features a Bearcat claw and the letter C. Thanks to his success on the court and the prominence of the Cincinnati basketball program, Bearcat apparel eventually became the number-two-selling national collegiate brand for Nike. When Bob Huggins left, all that went away.

The immediate benefactor was K-State. In previous seasons, K-State basketball had drawn on average about 5,800 season ticket holders to the 12,528-seat Bramlage Coliseum. Shortly after Huggins arrived, the team sold 11,000 season tickets, a sellout when you factor in allotments for student tickets. And even though he left after just one season, K-State sold out again in 2007–8. Before Huggins arrived in Manhattan, the last time K-State bas-ketball had had a sellout was 1982.

What was the economic impact of all this? Season ticket sales increased from $1.2 million to $2.7 million. Many of these season tickets were pur-chased by K-State's most avid—and wealthiest—boosters. In addition to buying basketball tickets, alumni donations to the basketball program in-creased a whopping $3 million under Huggins. That's nearly 8 percent of the school's total athletic budget.

Huggins also got K-State on national television for the first time in de-cades. That's important because the Big 12 Conference shares revenue pro-portionally. The more television time you have, the bigger your share of the Big 12's television revenue pie. Under Huggins, K-State made its first national television appearance in a game against Xavier. That one game alone earned K-State $135,000 in television money.

Before Huggins, most of K-State's games had only been broadcast re-gionally on Fox Sports Midwest. In 2006–7, the team appeared on ESPN more than a dozen times and on ABC twice. In 2007–8, more than half of K-State's regular-season games were seen on ESPN. And although the Old Spice and Jimmy V tournaments only pay expenses, both gave K-State bas-ketball more national television exposure and prestige than the program had had in decades.

In short, Huggins and K-State are a microcosm of the big business of college athletics. They're a prime example of what a winning program can do not only for a school's won-loss record but also for its finances. And that's what this book is all about: a sober look at the pluses and minuses of big-time college sports and what it has become as it has evolved from a million-dollar to a multibillion-dollar enterprise.

Money in college sports is nothing new, of course. Money has tainted college athletics since the day it began (although now, thanks to the U.S. Congress, donations to college athletics are tax-free). And although the U.S. Supreme Court ruled in 1984 that the NCAA's monopoly control of televi-sion rights amounted to an antitrust violation, it was a minor hiccup for the NCAA. What is new is the depth and breadth of influence, both finan-cial and otherwise, that college sports has within our culture. Furthermore, the corrupting influence of the big money that drives college athletics to-day reaches well beyond the college campus. It has infected every aspect of youth sports, from Little League to Amateur Athletic Union (AAU) basket-ball to Mighty Mites youth hockey leagues. The lure of big money—in the NCAA, as well as the NBA, NFL, and NHL—has corrupted youth sports to its very roots.

It is, I will argue over the following pages, this culture of superstardom above all else that has not only grown to historic proportions on our col-lege campuses but also infected high school and prep sports. It's a cultural degradation that, frankly, tells parents that it's OK to criticize—and some-times assault—youth coaches. It's a culture that drives parents to join Little League and Pop Warner organizing committees so that they can manipu-late the rosters to make sure that the right seven-year-olds are on the right team. It's a culture that tells parents it's OK to encourage their child to have reconstructive elbow surgery when he's fourteen so that he can be a better pitcher and maybe—just maybe—get a college scholarship. It's a culture that can dominate a family's entire life. It drives them to put everything else in their lives—other family matters, jobs, vacations—on hold. The sole focus of the family becomes supporting that "special kid" who they believe has a chance of making it.

What does "making it" mean today? Mostly it's about winning. Forget fundamentals. That's something the pasty-faced fat kids work on. For to-day's athletic superstars, be they eight or eighteen, it's about the culture of self. The culture of me. Or, viewed more broadly, the culture of self-promo-tion. It's about winning ball games, in hopes of getting noticed by the right coach, who will get you into the right camp, in front of the right scouts, and get you the right scholarship to the right school.

Again, forget the odds. The odds are for the other parents to worry about. Forget that just 3 percent of high school basketball players will get a Divi-sion I scholarship. And forget that less than 2 percent of those kids will have any kind of meaningful NBA career. These parents and their kids live in a culture of disbelief. Or, maybe I should say, a culture of belief. The parents each believe, with all their hearts and souls, that their kid is *the one*. The one who will defy the odds and become a superstar, with a multimillion-dollar contract, a multimillion-dollar house, a multimillion-dollar wife, his picture on a box of cereal, and a line of sporting goods with his name on it.

And what about the kids who don't make it? The kids who spend three, four, or five hours a day, from the time they're eight until they're eighteen, with one singular focus? The kids who play one sport and no others? The kids who get to 11th grade and don't want to go out for the team anymore because that's all they've been doing for the past ten years? We don't talk about them.

What could create such a sick and dysfunctional sports culture? Money. More money than college sports has ever seen before. And while money seems to be the singular focus of this subculture on our high school and college campuses, what about the kids? After all, they're what make all this possible. They have the talent that fills the seats, secures the television rights, and increases the alumni donations. What about them? They don't see a dime of this multibillion-dollar business (or at least they're not supposed to). In many ways, they're almost an afterthought. Why? Because they're an expendable commodity. A raw material that's in endless supply. And when they've outlived their usefulness, what happens to them? Most just go away, without a degree, never to be heard from again. They're expendable. Worse, they're disposable.

What does all this have to do with this book, and why should anyone read it? The short answer is that *Varsity Green* will cut through the clichés and common misconceptions and take a very clear-eyed look at the current state of college athletics. For instance, instead of ranting against (or defending) the ever-increasing budgets for college athletics, I'll explain what they mean. I'll explain that, yes, Ohio State has a $100 million athletic budget, and its teams play before sold-out stadiums every week. But I'll also tell you that Ohio State athletics spends nearly every cent that it brings in. In fact, the modest profit it earns is an anomaly, not the norm. Most college athletic programs—even many that are perceived to be successful and self-funding—are not self-sufficient. They rely on student activity fees, boosters, and other sources of off-field revenue to keep them in the black.

There is an increasing body of evidence that suggests that the basketball team is being funded at the expense of the biology department. According to the *Chronicle of Higher Education,* for decades academic donations far outpaced those to athletics. That is starting to change. Athletic donations continue to rise, while academic giving has remained flat. That's important because it's a sign—one sign—that in some instances athletics is starting to eclipse academics.

Equally as important as the economics of college athletics are the human factors. College sports, like any human endeavor, are made up of people. Some of their stories are tragic. Some are heroic, almost mythical. But in the end, what this book will explain is that for all the billion-dollar business decisions that are made in college sports today, they ultimately affect people: players, coaches, parents, boosters, administrators, officials, and fans.

Throughout this book, I will look at the major issues of the day that are affecting college athletics. I will talk about how these issues have an impact on the economics of a business—and that's what it is, a business—that seems to know no bounds. More important, I will look at how these decisions affect the people who toil in this business every day.

I'll start with a brief history of college sports. You may be surprised to learn that there never was an age of innocence. College athletics has been driven by money from the day it started.

I'll look at the so-called "facilities arms race." Much of the national focus has been on the intense contest between Michigan, Ohio State, and Penn State to see who can build the biggest football stadium and pack it with the most avid fans every autumn weekend. But you may be surprised to learn that this mine-is-bigger-than-yours battle goes much deeper into the NCAA landscape than the schools that get national television coverage every week.

The debate over coaches' salaries is renewed every time a new record is set. Critics often argue that there must be something wrong when the coach makes more than the chemistry professor, the college president, or the governor. But what may surprise you is how those salaries are paid. Today, only about 25 percent of a coach's salary is paid by the university. The biggest chunk comes from sponsors, especially broadcasters, who seem to have an unlimited budget when it comes to paying for sports broadcasting rights.

I'll look at graduation rates, which are in the spotlight again with the

NCAA's new Academic Progress Rate measurement. Contrary to popular belief, most athletic departments have graduation rates that are about on par with the rest of the student body. The idea that they don't is a common misperception unwittingly facilitated by a lazy media culture that doesn't have the time, the energy, or the curiosity to look past the clichés.

When Kansas State basketball standout Michael Beasley threw his hat in the ring for the NBA draft, it was breaking news. What the media doesn't report about are the thousands of kids who aren't Division I athletes who leave school every year, for a variety of reasons. Like star athletes, some of these students never return to finish. And you'll meet the academic advisers and athletic directors who work hard to get the kids into school, and then try to keep them there.

I'll take a look at the AAU system, which is a wholly owned subsidiary of the shoe companies and, many argue, irreparably broken. It ranks kids as young as nine, encourages a cult of personality instead of teamwork and fundamentals, and sets unrealistic—and unhealthy—goals and expectations for athletes who are too young, too focused, and too self-absorbed. The NCAA and the NBA have vowed to fix youth basketball, but they are the two entities that have gained the most from the commercialization of youth basketball. Therefore, are they the right partners to fix this dysfunctional system?

And, of course, with athletic success comes pressure. Pressure to recruit. Pressure to sell tickets. And pressure to always win.

Sometimes the pressure gets to be too much. Coaches direct academically unprepared athletes to the "cake courses," where they're guaranteed the C that will maintain their NCAA eligibility. Sometimes coaches look the other way and ignore a player's abhorrent—sometimes criminal—off-court behavior. And, sometimes, players are paid under the table.

You'll also meet the reformers. The people, such as University of Oregon professor Nathan Tublitz, who argue that college athletics is broken beyond repair and is doing grave harm to the academic integrity of today's colleges and universities.

Which brings us back to our original question: Why did Kansas State president Jon Wefald take the risk of hiring Bob Huggins? To sell some tickets, please some alumni, and see his team on television. That should tell you something about the current state of college athletics and the sway it can hold over coaches, college presidents, students, athletes, and alumni.

"With big bucks dangling before their eyes, many NCAA schools find the temptations of success too alluring to worry about the rules," said noted sports economist Andrew Zimbalist. "Schools cheat. They cheat by arranging to help their prospective athletes pass standardized tests. They cheat by providing illegal payments to their recruits. They cheat by setting up special rinky-dink curricula so their athletes can stay qualified. And when one school cheats, others feel compelled to do the same."

The NCAA, always racing to catch up, keeps passing more rules, hoping to curtail it all.

"Sometimes these rules are enforced, sometimes not," Zimbalist said. "But rarely is the penalty harsh enough to be a serious deterrent. The solution, it turns out, is more rules."

1 THE ENTERTAINMENT PRODUCT

The most refreshing—and honest—person I met while researching this book is Phil Hughes, the associate athletic director for student services at Kansas State University. He clearly has no illusions about his job. And you may not like what he has to say.

"My job is to protect The Entertainment Product," he stated matter-of-factly. "My job is to make sure that The Entertainment Product goes to class. My job is to make sure that The Entertainment Product studies. My job is to make sure that The Entertainment Product makes adequate academic progress according to NCAA guidelines."

What he calls "The Entertainment Product," much of the rest of the world calls "the student-athlete." The former phrase is brutally honest; the latter part of the phalanx of lies and half-truths that provide the bulwark of the façade of amateurism that falsely cloaks college athletics. Hughes's characterization may sound harsh, but is, in fact, the reality. Rather than scorn him, we should all be grateful for his candor.

"It's how I sleep at night," Hughes said. "It is who and what these kids are. You can hate that, you can hate the system. But at the end of the day, it's who they are. They're the raw material in a multibillion-dollar sports and entertainment business. And it's my job to protect them."

Once you get past the shock of Hughes's blunt characterization of the kids he oversees every day, you realize that he's absolutely right. He's also an anomaly. That's because he's a rare voice of sanity and honesty amid a nationwide army of academic advisers and tutors on campuses across the country who cajole, coddle, and coach these kids, most of whom have no business being at a serious institution of advanced academic learning. Some of these academic advisers are also fighting their own institutions, which are more concerned with an athlete's academic eligibility and ability to sell tickets than whether or not he or she is passing freshman English.

STUDENTS FIRST, ATHLETES SECOND?

University presidents will tell you that the kids are "students first and athletes second," but that's a canard. In reality, most of these kids are, as Hughes calls them, "The Entertainment Product." They're the raw material—the talent—that draws millions of avid fans to collegiate stadiums and arenas across the country every week. That is the cold harsh reality of the business of college sports today.

Given that, Phil Hughes is not a monster. He's a realist.

A 1980 graduate of the University of California, San Diego, Hughes has a master's degree in counseling psychology from the University of Kentucky. And while he may sound like he's part of the problem, he is, in fact, just a realist. For better or worse, he accepts his role as a small cog in a very big moneymaking machine.

Hughes has been at this game for a long time. In 2009, he was entering his thirteenth year at Kansas State. Before that, he was at the University of Michigan for seven years, responsible for the athletic department's student-athlete support program, which includes academic advising, academic compliance, tutorial services, admissions tracking, faculty relations, and something called "academic advocacy."

Hughes's office at Kansas State is in the $1 million Academic Learning Center. It's part of the Vanier Complex, the $2 million football facility that Kansas State built in 1992. It includes locker rooms, a 6,500-square-foot weight room, an athletic training room, a players' lounge, and the Big Eight Room, a plush lounge where Kansas State signs some of its most-promising recruits.

In addition to Hughes, there are six full-time counselors, six assistant counselors and grad assistants, and a tutoring staff of about forty-five serving four hundred athletes. Among the services offered to K-State athletes are academic advising and counseling; tutoring; assistance with writing skills, time management, goal setting, and computer skills; a faculty mentoring program; and supervised study time. The athletes also have faculty advisers in their chosen major. With the exception of the faculty adviser, there are small-group tutorial aids that are otherwise unavailable to students who aren't scholarship athletes. Remarkably, despite the individual attention, many of these athletes never come close to graduating. But as is the case on hundreds of campuses across the country, Hughes and the administration pretend that is their goal.

"My number one goal is keeping our kids grounded in the business at hand, which is competing successfully in the classroom," Hughes said. "It's a very nuts-and-bolts activity. Kid gets up, feet hit the floor, and that kid has to make progress in their academic commitments and obligations, *that day*. And it's trench work. That's what we talk with our kids about."

While some see these personalized tutoring services as merely another example of the special treatment athletes are accorded their whole lives, Hughes understands the academic quality of the raw material he's been given to work with. These kids may be gifted athletes, but many are sorely lacking in not only academic discipline but the very rudimentary knowledge that a high school education is supposed to provide. That's because many of them have been passed along through the grades from teacher to teacher, all tacitly acknowledging that these kids weren't born to learn, they were born to play.

Recognizing the academic shortcomings of many of his athletes, Hughes does what he can while he has the kids. And although some may see it as special treatment, Hughes takes the very pragmatic view that it would be crueler to bring kids to a university the size and stature of Kansas State and give them all the tools they need to succeed on the playing field but then leave them to fend for themselves in the classroom.

"We put ourselves in close proximity to the athlete to achieve that very singular goal," he said. "And that goal is day-to-day progress in their academic requirements."

Fighting Hughes and his staff all the way—even in non-revenue sports such as equestrianism and rowing—is an army of adults who have only one thing in mind: winning. This group often includes parents, coaches, mentors, and friends.

"So many of the adults only want to focus on and talk about the next match. Where do they rank?" Hughes said. "That's what these kids have heard their whole life. We have to be the adults who say, 'How did you do on that chemistry test?'"

TWO FULL-TIME JOBS

At Kansas State, the academic advisers try to stress the importance of academics as soon as the athletes arrive on campus. In fact, many incoming freshmen come to school in June or July for minicamps and begin taking classes right away, in hopes that the light load of a summer session will better prepare them for the full course load they're expected to take in the fall.

"What we tell recruits is that being a student-athlete is like having two full-time jobs," Hughes said. "We alert them and their parents to the difficulty in choosing this type of pathway."

The athletes will have three to five hours less per day to study than other students, he continued, "because their second job—sports—commands so much time and energy. Other students can work part-time, arrange their own schedule. These students are told, 'Here's what the deal is: Lift at six A.M. Practice from three to six P.M. Go to classes in between. And study group here at seven P.M.'"

Hughes said that his department has to offer student-athletes so many tutorial services because practice and training for their sport takes up so much of their day.

"We tell recruits to look at the kids in their class to the right and left of them. They have five hours more a day to study than you do. How do you compete? That's what we're here to help them do.

"We take so much of their mental and physical energy," he pointed out, referring to the athletic department. "They have to study with us after they're beat up, tired, or just plain exhausted.

"Like it or not, these kids are elite athletes. "It is the institution that chooses to be a member of the NCAA. Once you've made that decision, in order to compete athletically or in the entertainment business, you have to support these students so that they can survive and hopefully succeed academically."

How exactly do they do that?

"We make sure that their schedule fits their interests and abilities," Hughes answered. "We will work with them to solve any problems and any distractions that take away from that daily progress. We will monitor their academic standing and their academic performance. We offer tutorial and mentoring services. And we act as advocates with the university."

While some may see that as coddling, Hughes feels that regardless of the help his staff gives to the athletes, at the end of the day it's up to the individual athlete whether or not he or she succeeds in the classroom.

"My program has no academic authority, and that's a good thing," he affirmed. "Academic authority is retained in the university. My signature doesn't mean anything. I don't grant degrees. Student-athletes have to follow the procedures and protocols of every other student."

Maybe so, but they definitely are getting more hands-on attention than many other students. For instance, all new athletes actually have a study partner, someone on Hughes's staff who sits with them and does their homework with them ("but not for them," he insists).

"We do that in order for us to get to know our students," Hughes said. "We need to watch them study. We need to talk with them. How'd you like Spanish? How'd you do in Lit class? We have to gauge their level of motivation, anticipation, and their level of commitment. So we need to be with them."

While Hughes and his staff are available to the athletes twenty-four hours a day, each team sets its own study-time requirements. One team may want athletes to have six hours of required study time per week. Others might only require four. Some student-athletes are self-motivated, whereas others may require significant handholding.

For instance, Kansas State has a program called the Study Table, common at many universities. Not only does it set a rigid schedule of what subject student-athletes will study and for how long, it also checks up on them between classes.

"As we do our initial screening of our student-athletes, we will assign them, based on need, to our daytime program," Hughes described. "Before class, between class, and after class they meet with tutors or academic mentors, and they get their work done during the day, while they have the energy and the focus to do it."

In addition to tutoring, Hughes's staff conducts review sessions, helps athletes prepare for midterm and final exams, and offers one-on-one tutoring sessions.

"We do have tutors available in the evening, and we have tutors on call," Hughes said. "But again, this is a day-to-day slog. So we've found that it works best if the tutoring is done on a regular, scheduled, consistent basis. Our goal is to offer daily tutoring, not end-of-semester cramming."

All freshmen get tutoring whether they think they need it or not. And it continues, "until they prove to us that they can handle the quality and quantity of work."

ECONOMICS VERSUS ACADEMICS

While Hughes's focus is supposed to be on academics, the economics of college athletics are never very far from his mind. They have to be, because that is the world in which the student-athletes live. Moreover, regardless of any legitimate concern Hughes may have for these kids, their ultimate focus, their whole reason for being on campus, is to keep the multibillion-dollar college sports machine running.

"My customers are an Entertainment Product that resides within a seventeen- to twenty-two-year-old person," Hughes acknowledged. "And that is a crazy proposition."

The greatest threat to that Entertainment Product is when they get arrested, test positive for steroids or street drugs, or get caught taking money from boosters.

"It's a very fragile existence for our business and for that youngster," said Hughes. "The problem at K-State, Ohio State, Michigan is that these young athletes are treated like celebrities by their peers. They are granted great status, and they have great distractions. Many youngsters seventeen to twenty-two don't handle that type of attention or status very well. Poor social and personal decisions are what make this whole NCAA business really tenuous. And we've constructed this elaborate entertainment industry with this cast of actors and actresses.

"And if you think about the developmental issues of young people in college, regardless of whether or not they're an athlete, those challenges are *huge*, period. Then you throw them in front of seventy-five thousand screaming fans, add in the travel and the intensity of the competition, and prospects of the Olympics or pro sports.

"If you think of the threats to an athletic department, the things that can bring down the house. If you're losing and have to fire the coach, that's part of the equation. That's anticipated and expected. It doesn't kill you. What can kill you is the behavioral decisions of the athlete. Gambling. Sexually assaulting someone."

Going back to his use of the term *Entertainment Product,* Hughes, again, has a very real-world view of the world of college athletics.

"The NCAA entertainment business is really founded on two concepts," he said. "All of these kids are amateurs. So amateurism is the cornerstone of this entertainment business. They're here for the love of the school."

The second is integrity.

"Integrity and amateurism. It's a house of cards," Hughes commented. "All of the NCAA legislation is based on maintaining these two false premises. You have seventeen- to twenty-two-year-old students who don't fit into those parameters and can become a threat."

So how does Phil Hughes, an otherwise upstanding, decent guy, keep his sanity amid this crazy system that says it's about academics but is really about maintaining the economic viability of college athletics?

"You accept it for what it is," he said. "That's all you can do. I'm trying to make an impossible equation work. It's a dogfight every day. I relish when we can make it work."

On the upside, Hughes considers it progress that academic tutoring facilities are now part of the so-called "facilities arms race," in which schools try to outdo each other to build the most luxurious, state-of-the-art sports facilities. The trend, admittedly, is partly fueled by ego—"My stadium is bigger and nicer than yours." But mostly these facilities are used in the battle to lure recruits, thus the term *facilities arms race*. Put more simply, if I'm the coach at a school that has a training center with underwater treadmills, the newest sports-medicine treatments and techniques, and a weight room with seventy Nautilus machines, then maybe I can convince a recruit to choose my school over another that has only sixty-five Nautilus machines and no underwater treadmills.

"At one point, I delivered academic support services out of a double-wide trailer," Hughes said. "I referred to it as our mobile academic unit. The buildings we're seeing today for academic tutoring are a marked change from what they were just ten years ago."

In addition to new facilities, Division I schools also are increasingly adding staff, including people like Hughes, who do nothing but make sure that student-athletes are working hard at maintaining their NCAA-mandated academic eligibility. In other words, at almost every college and university across the country, Hughes has a counterpart, worrying about the same problems that he does.

NOTRE DAME DOES IT BEST

These athletic tutoring programs are not really new, they've simply grown in size and stature over the years. Not surprisingly, the University of Notre Dame, one of the few schools where athletes have a higher graduation rate than the general student body, started the first full-fledged student-athlete tutoring center, in 1964.

"Father Joyce saw what was happening with television," said Mike De-Cicco, who started the Notre Dame program and retired as the assistant athletic director for academic advisement in 1995. "He knew that television would not only bring greater exposure to college football, but also greater scrutiny."

It's that increased scrutiny, from the NCAA and every once in a while from the media, that has motivated schools to build these lavish academic tutoring centers. That way, when the starting tackle flunks out, the school can point to the million-dollar facility and say, "We gave him every opportunity." For the most part, college sports writers are all too willing to accept that explanation and move on. In reality, the few instances of academic fraud that are reported every year are the tip of the iceberg, not examples of the effectiveness of the NCAA's policing policies or the investigative reporting skills of sycophantic sports writers.

Notre Dame is one of the few exceptions when it comes to big-time Division I athletic programs. Whereas other schools have been dragged kicking and screaming into this new era of academic accountability, Notre Dame has long been committed to the academic success of its student-athletes.

But in 1964, it was a very different world for Mike DeCicco, a Notre Dame grad who'd come back to South Bend to teach mechanical engineering and thermodynamics, and to coach the fencing team. That's when Father Joyce, the school's legendary executive vice president, called DeCicco into his office and asked him to set up a program to monitor the academic progress of the football team.

"At most," DeCicco said, "Father Joyce figured it would take an hour or two a day."

Unsure of where to start, DeCicco began by calling the athletic directors at the Ivy League and Big Ten schools his fencers competed against.

"I called and asked them if there was someone I could talk to about academic advising for student-athletes," DeCicco recalled. "Not one of them said they had anyone other than a coach who might work with the admissions office to make sure that their kids would get in. That sort of thing. There was nothing along the line of what Father Joyce had in mind."

Next, DeCicco called the other conferences. They weren't any help, either.

"The closest thing I came to what I was looking for was at the University of Texas," he said. "They had an assistant coach they called 'The brain coach.' They said he worked with the admissions office, knew who the coaches wanted to bring in, and made sure that the kids got in and then kept records of them to find out if any of them were flunking out. I talked to him and he didn't have any academic contact with the student-athletes as far as their majors, grade point average, and so on."

So DeCicco essentially had to create the Notre Dame athlete-tutoring program from scratch. He started by calling every football player into his office and asking them a few key questions. What courses were they taking? What was their major? What was their grade-point average?

One football player in particular, an Academic All-American who went on to have a successful NFL and legal career, assured DeCicco that he was passing all his courses.

A week after the interviews was Notre Dame's Mid-Semester Report Day. That's when the school sent out pink slips to every student who was failing a class. DeCicco had reassured Father Joyce that the football players were all doing well in their classes, but he wanted to double-check. So he asked the Registrar's Office to send him copies of the mid-term grades for all the football players. He didn't expect to get them until later in the afternoon, but when he came into his office that morning, sitting on his desk was a stack of pink slips an inch and a half high. On top was the pink-slip report for the football player who'd assured DeCicco that he was passing all his classes. In reality, he had a D and an F in two of his five classes.

"I was so dejected that I simply locked the door to my office and came home," DeCicco said. "I said to my wife, 'Honey, I may be the shortest-tenured academic adviser in Christiandom.'"

When he told his wife what had happened, she said, "Don't ask the kids, ask the teachers."

The next day, DeCicco was called into Father Joyce's office.

"Mike, I thought you had told me that everyone was doing so well," Father Joyce said over the top of his signature half-moon reading glasses.

"It didn't take an intellectual giant to recognize that it was Father Joyce who'd put the stack of pink slips on my desk," DeCicco said.

A UNIVERSITY-WIDE EFFORT

That was the first—and last—time that DeCicco was called into Father Joyce's office about the poor academic performance of any student-athletes. The next day, DeCicco took his wife's advice and began enlisting the help of the Notre Dame faculty in keeping track of student grades. The program was so successful that DeCicco's one-man operation soon ballooned to a staff of five. Today, Notre Dame is considered the gold standard when it comes to balancing athletics and academics.

"Some kids were flunking because they couldn't do the work," DeCicco said. "It wasn't that they weren't smart enough, but they were spending so much time memorizing the playbook and practicing and traveling to away games that it was almost impossible to keep up with their school work."

He said he was lucky enough to have deans and department heads who recommended students who could tutor the athletes.

"We ended up having sixty or seventy tutors, most of them graduate students who were looking for an extra buck or two," he said. "We had small-group tutoring, as well as one-on-one."

DeCicco also credits coaches, such as Notre Dame's Ara Parseghian, for making the academic tutoring program work.

"The success of our program, aside from getting the information we needed and keeping the kids on track, was dependent upon the coaches we had at that time," DeCicco said. "One of the concerns I had was what kind of cooperation was I going to get from the coaches. I was naïve enough to think that all the kids we recruited and brought in were intellectual giants, as well as good athletes. But that wasn't the case."

By the time DeCicco's first class of tutored athletes graduated, the kid who'd had the two pink slips graduated with honors and was drafted by the Minnesota Vikings. A few years later, he came back to Notre Dame to finish his law degree. He brought two teammates with him from the Vikings who hadn't completed their undergraduate work at Michigan State. And their first stop was DeCicco's office.

"They were indicative of what was going on in college football then," DeCicco said. "Too many young men were finishing their eligibility and had not completed their degree requirements."

While it's true that graduation rates are not what they should be for all students, the majority of the problem seems to be with young black kids who shouldn't have been admitted in the first place. DeCicco deserves credit for starting a program that has been copied in one form or another at every major university across the country.

"We started by telling the kids that they had to go to class," he said. "We told them that they had to take courses designed to meet their academic requirements. As a result, we had a very high graduation rate among our athletes. And still do. And it's because of the support Notre Dame gave me. The coaches, the faculty, the administration, and Father Joyce. I had the authority to pull kids off the field."

A few years after he started the athlete tutoring and mentoring program for the football team, DeCicco expanded it to include every varsity sport. When Title IX went into effect in 1972, academic support services were extended to women's teams. It has since been expanded to support staff, such as team managers, trainers, and graduate assistants.

"Every sport had one or two kids who needed tutoring help," DeCicco said. "Even some of my fencers, who overall were pretty smart kids."

Notre Dame also started offering summer-school classes and tutoring to help its student-athletes get up to speed before the start of their freshman semester. But the first year, DeCicco had just six kids sign up.

"They thought summer school was for dummies," he said. "I told them that it wasn't. That given all the time commitments they had to athletics, they needed a leg up, a head start on the other kids. When I explained it that way, they started to come."

Today, summer school is required for Notre Dame pre-med students and others who enter particularly challenging disciplines—whether or not they're athletes. Eventually, the summer tutoring program became so popular that Notre Dame had to cap it.

"Every school needs an academic advising program," said DeCicco. "It just makes sense, no matter how prepared or unprepared the kids are."

Today, Notre Dame's Academic Services for Student-Athletes is housed in the 67,000-square-foot, $14 million Coleman-Morse Center. The school is ranked second all-time in the number of academic All-Americans it has produced. And virtually every major D-I program in the country has a program just like the one Mike DeCicco started at Notre Dame forty years ago.

Student-athletes at the University of Georgia study in a $7 million facility funded by and named for Rankin M. Smith, a long-time booster and former owner of the Atlanta Falcons. It's 31,000 square feet, has a 230-seat study hall, twenty tutoring rooms, sixty computer stations, and a writing lab. It has a nearly $1 million annual budget to pay for ten full-time staffers and about eighty graduate-assistant tutors.

The University of Michigan recently spent about $15 million on a new student-athlete academic tutoring center. Texas A&M spent nearly $10 million. Richard Lapchick, director of the Institute of Diversity and Ethics in Sport at the University of Central Florida, said in the Winter 2004 newsletter for the National Center for Public Policy and Higher Education that these centers send "a message to the student-athletes . . . that this is a priority; they're not just building football facilities. They're building these centers to help you become intelligent students—not just student-athletes."

At least that's the company line.

NOT THE BEST OF INTENTIONS

Sometimes the tutoring centers are used to cover up academic shortcomings, not cure them. In the early 1980s, when Herschel Walker was breaking SEC and NCAA rushing records at Georgia, the school was also breaking the rules. Instead of having tutors help the student-athletes study, they were actually doing their work for them. The whistleblower was Jan Kemp, a remedial studies teacher who refused to change grades for athletes to maintain their NCAA eligibility. She eventually won a $2.5 million lawsuit against the university, which fired her for exposing the widespread academic fraud.

What won the case for Kemp was a secret tape she introduced during the trial, which featured her boss, Leroy Ervin, telling staffers, "I know for a fact that these kids would not be here if it were not for their utility to the institution. They are used as a kind of raw material in the production of some goods to be sold as whatever product, and they get nothing in return."

Vince Dooley, the Bulldogs' head football coach and athletic director who, despite being at the center of the scandal, kept his job, testified that athletes were admitted with SAT scores of less than 650 out of a possible 1,600.

"In order to be, we think, reasonably competitive, we thought that leeway was necessary," he said in his own defense.

Fast forward to March 10, 1999, the day before the number seven seed Minnesota Golden Gophers were to open the NCAA Tournament against number ten Gonzaga. The *St. Paul Pioneer Press* reported allegations of massive academic fraud in the men's basketball program. Former basketball office manager Jan Gangelhoff went to the paper and claimed that she had written over four hundred papers for at least twenty Gopher men's basketball players. The university suspended players Antoine Broxie, Kevin Clark, Jason Stanford, and Miles Tarver. All allegedly had had papers written for them by Gangelhoff in previous seasons.

The university negotiated a buyout of men's basketball coach Clem Haskins's contract, worth a reported $1.5 million dollars over three years. A year later, Haskins admitted that he had paid Gangelhoff $3,000 for tutoring services. He also turned his financial records over to the NCAA. By the time the investigation was completed, it was also learned that Haskins had tampered with transcripts for incoming recruits, given cash payments to players, ignored complaints of sexual harrassment against his players, and tried to convince professors to give his players inflated grades. The University of Minnesota men's basketball team was stripped of all awards and titles dating back to the 1993–94 season. The school lost five scholarships over the next three seasons, had its recruiting limited, and was on NCAA probation for four years. In addition to Haskins, other members of his athletic staff also resigned. The university returned 90 percent (about $350,000) of the profits earned by the basketball program during its appearances in the NCAA tournament, including the team's 1997 Final Four run.

And, of course, in 2008 we had the Florida State online music quiz scandal. To recap: about thirty Florida State football players, along with nonathletes, cheated on an online, open-book music exam. Graduate assistants who administerd the test directed students to a Web site where they could find the answers to all the questions. Ironically, these athletes were barred from going to the Music City Bowl in Nashville, where one of the free giveaways to players was an MP3 player.

MEDIA DISTORTION

While these schools were clearly cheating and deserved the punishments that were meted out, I think it's also fair to say that there's some media distortion when it comes to these academic scandals. Every minor transgression committed by a student-athlete that is reported is almost guaranteed to receive front-page coverage in the local paper, and is broadcast nationwide by the wire services and the twenty-four-hour all-sports stations. This has two effects. It makes it seem as though there are more scandals than there actually are, and it allows the otherwise fawning sports editors and talking heads to declare that they cover the bad, as well as the good, of athletics.

According to newspaper research, 85 percent of American males open to the sports page first. According to the University of Oregon, about 70 percent of its media mentions were sports-related. The remainder were alumni and faculty obituaries.

It's also important to point out that there are other students on campus besides athletes who receive what could be considered special treatment. The general public usually doesn't read about these kids because the local paper and the national networks don't cover, for example, the Indiana School of Music and Dance as closely as they do Indiana basketball.

A good case in point is Grace McLoughlin, a name that I'm sure doesn't ring any bells with 99 percent of you reading this book. At 5'7" and 120 pounds, she was one of the top recruits in the country in 2008. She's been practicing her discipline since she was four. She has spent nearly every summer at elite camps and has traveled across the country to perform and train. Is she a gymnast? A swimmer? One of the growing number of high-profile women's lacrosse players? No, she's a ballerina.

In early 2008, she was being wooed heavily by the University of Indiana's Jacobs School of Music, one of the most prestigious performance arts programs in the country. Yet while the press corps for the entire state of Indiana was busy writing about the recruiting scandal surrounding Indiana men's basketball coach Kelvin Sampson, what went mostly unnoticed was the hiring of Michael Vernon as chairman of Indiana's ballet department.

Vernon is easily as important to the world of ballet as Sampson is to the world of basketball.

Michael Vernon studied at the Nesta Brooking School of Ballet and the Royal Ballet School in London. Before coming to New York in 1976 to join the Eglevsky Ballet as a ballet master and resident choreographer, he performed regularly with the Royal Ballet, the Royal Opera Ballet, and the London Festival Ballet.

Vernon continues to teach classes at New York–based Steps, works regularly for the Manhattan Dance Project, and is artistic adviser to the Ballet School of Stamford. Since 2000, he has taught and choreographed the ballet company and ballet school at the Chautauqua Institute in western upstate New York. These are some of the camps and companies where Grace McLoughlin has danced for Vernon, and he is the reason she applied to the Jacobs school.

Of course, you didn't read about Ms. McLoughlin or Mr. Vernon on the front page of the *Indianapolis Star* or even the *Bloomington Herald Times*. That's because they don't fill thirty-thousand-seat arenas and generate millions of dollars in television revenue for the school. But looking at what could arguably be conceived as the privileged world that McLoughlin inhabited (she ultimately ended up dancing in Los Angeles), her high school class schedule and the special treatment she received weren't much different than those accorded to star football and basketball players.

She went to the exclusive Performance Children's School on Manhattan's Upper West Side, which is purposely just steps from the Juilliard School of Music and Lincoln Center. She was part of the Guided Study program, which allows gifted performers to have tailor-made schedules to accommodate their practice sessions and performances.

"I can only be in school about three periods a day, and I have six classes," she said. "So a lot of times I take a class and never actually attend class in school. I meet teachers after school, take tests online."

If she were the starting forward for Erasmus Hall High School in Brooklyn, those revelations alone would be worthy of a front-page expose in the *New York Times*. But because she was a ballerina and not a ballplayer, as a society we're not as appalled.

McLoughlin wasn't alone. The Performance Children's School has dozens of students who are accomplished actors, actresses, dancers, and musicians. And they're all accorded the sort of academic freedom and flexibility that McLoughlin had.

"A lot of the kids are equestrians who leave school from December to May to do the Florida circuit," she said. "They get all their assignments online and turn in their homework by e-mail."

Another one of her classmates composed the score for the 2008 Summer Olympics in Beijing.

On a typical Monday, McLoughlin went to school for just two periods—Advanced Physics and English—and then walked five blocks to dance for a few hours. She went back to school late in the afternoon to meet with teachers and catch up on her assignments.

When she wasn't dancing in a show with one of the local dance companies, she spent about fifteen hours a week in dance classes outside of school.

"That doesn't include Pilates classes or seminars," she said. "During rehearsals or workshops, I add about two hours a day to my dance schedule and three hours on Saturday."

All of her homework assignments were posted online.

"Sometimes I go in to take a test, but the teachers are pretty great about extensions and giving me as much time as I need," she said.

Again, if McLoughlin were a student-athlete and this story came out, her face would have been plastered on the front of every sports section in the country. The headlines would have read "Only Goes to Half Her Classes" or "Spends More Time Practicing Than in School."

My point is not to dismiss the special treatment that athletes get. The job of starting quarterback or point guard at a major Division I university comes with privileges and special accommodations that every freshman would love to have, including personalized one-on-one tutoring. My point is that for all that is wrong with college athletics today and the star status it gives to its top players, there is a media magnifying glass that inflates every academic transgression by a student-athlete that is uncovered. And oftentimes, the coverage is disproportionate to the crime. One of the reasons I think these episodes are so distorted is to give cover to lazy sports reporters who not only don't work very hard at uncovering NCAA academic and recruiting violations but couldn't care less whether or not the student-athletes had the minimal SAT scores and grades that were required of every other student, or are passing remedial English that should have been taught in junior high. In fact, I would argue that many of these sports reporters who are turning a blind eye to corruption and cheating are actually aiding and abetting what's essentially a criminal enterprise. Furthermore, it is the six or ten pages of daily sports coverage in newspapers that is part of the media frenzy that actually helps schools cash such big checks for media rights and endorsement deals.

It's all part of the dysfunctional system of college athletics. And while today the money is bigger and more influential than ever, this atmosphere has been around since the earliest days of college athletics.

2 AN INAUSPICIOUS BEGINNING

The first thing you should realize is that there never was a "golden age" of college athletics. It never existed. There never was a time when it was all about virginal cheerleaders in tight-fitting sweaters that never came off in the back seats of cars. Pep rallies were never just about school spirit. Playing your best and demonstrating good sportsmanship never supplanted the ultimate goal of winning. In short, college athletics has been corrupt since the day it was born.

The curriculum at most colleges and universities has included some sort of physical fitness regimen since the day they opened their doors. The Ivy League schools copied the model that was used at the elite boarding schools in England. Sometimes these athletic activities included inter-squad scrimmages in track and field, rugby, and a brutish form of European soccer that eventually became known as American football.

The most violent form of the game was played in the early 19th century on the first Monday of every fall term at Harvard. The sophomores would play the freshmen in a soccer-style football game that became known as Bloody Monday.

"The game consisted of two opposing gangs of as many as 100 boys alternately rushing toward or running away from one another with no thought in mind other than to injure the opposing class as much as possible," wrote Francis X. Dealy Jr. in his excellent book, *Win at Any Cost.*

ROWING

Many sports historians peg the start of organized intercollegiate athletics to the 1852 rowing contest between Harvard and Yale on New Hampshire's

Lake Winnipesaukee. Why not Boston's Charles River? Because, like much of college athletics today, the event was a commercial endeavor first and an athletic competition second.

The match was the brainchild of James Elkins, superintendent of the Boston-Concord-Montreal Railroad. Billed as a rowing event, it really was meant to increase ridership on the railroad. Both teams were given free transportation, along with lavish gifts and unlimited alcohol. The several thousand spectators who followed the teams to the New Hampshire countryside—arguably America's first boosters—paid their own way.

Both teams were so drunk by the start of the race that it's a wonder they could compete. The contest had to be delayed an hour so they could sober up. The Harvard squad did this best, and rowed its shell, *Oneida*, across the finish line ten lengths ahead of Yale. Presidential aspirant General Franklin Pierce was in attendance, and presented the Harvard rowers with prizes valued at more than $500, including gold-leafed oars and jeweled trophies from Tiffany & Co.

This contest—and the under-the-table money surrounding it—is emblematic of the world of college athletics in the 19th and early 20th century. That world was dominated by the Ivy League, and the sport of choice was football. Today, of course, the Ivy League has been relegated to second-class citizenship in the high-dollar world of college athletics. Unlike its more-monied, more-commercial, and more-successful rivals in the Big Ten and the SEC, the Ivy League actually expects its athletes to be students first and athletes second. The starting quarterback at Cornell and the left guard at Dartmouth not only have to have serious SAT scores and solid high school grades in real classes such as trigonometry and advance placement physics, they're also expected to pursue a serious college major. But in the mid- to late-19th century, long before the Ivy League eschewed the corrupting influence of athletic scholarships and postseason bowl money, the Harvard-Yale rivalry was the most intense in the country.

In the 1860s, as many as twenty-five thousand spectators would line the banks of the Charles River to watch a Harvard-Yale crew race. The race was almost an afterthought. The event was a collegiate bacchanalia akin to the toga party in *Animal House*. There was heavy drinking and taunting cheers and jeers, and betting was rampant. It was, in short, a complete departure from the English boarding school system that these events were designed to mimic. The U.S. collegiate rivalries quickly devolved into something very different. While the English saw sport as a healthy way to build strong bodies along with strong minds, in America sports quickly became—for many—all that mattered on college campuses.

"America was too free-wheeling and too competitive for its colleges to continue the chivalrous British tradition of playing sport for fun," wrote Dealy. "The stride America had made, when applied to intercollegiate athletics, meant an all-or-nothing preoccupation with winning. The Harvard-Yale competition, for example, determined far more than which school had the fastest shell. Judging from the intensity of the spectators and the participants, the stakes included which school had the more beautiful campus, the smarter faculty, the brighter student body and the more successful alumni."

Nineteenth-century Harvard philosophy professor George Santayana echoed these sentiments when he said, "In athletics, as in all performances, only winning is interesting. The rest has value only as leading to it or reflecting it."

In 1855, three years after that first commercial collegiate sports spectacle on Lake Winnipesaukee, the first known college athletic eligibility violation occurred. The Harvard coxswain was an alumnus, not a student.

Despite the culture of corruption that surrounded college sports from its very inception, college presidents and alumni associations quickly embraced athletics as a way to spread the name and enhance the reputations of their schools, and to curry alumni favor and donations. In other words, from 1855 in New England to 2007 in Manhattan, Kansas, not much has changed.

"[You have] done more to make Columbia known than all your predecessors," President Harry Barnard told the Columbia crew team after an important victory. "Little was known about Columbia one month ago," he said, "but today wherever the telegraph cable extends, the existence of Columbia College is known and respected."

BASEBALL

The first intercollegiate baseball game took place in 1859. Amherst beat Williams, 73 to 32.

During the Civil War, Confederate and Union soldiers often played baseball to pass the "hurry up and wait" hours that are common in the military—even in wartime. After the war, those that still had all their limbs took their love of baseball to the college campus. By the end of the 1860s, college baseball held the same prominence as Major League Baseball does today. As a result, no one said a word a decade later when Lee Richmond helped Brown beat Yale, 3 to 2, in the 1878 college championships. Richmond was a professional player with the Worcester Sentinels. Harvard's Walter Clarkson was also a pro baseball player who regularly suited up for college games. Only after he helped the Crimson beat Yale five times did the Harvard Athletic Committee throw him off the team.

The Ivy League schools not only used professional players, they protected their students' academic eligibility by creating special schools and courses just for them. For instance, many Harvard players attended the "scientific school," which, despite the name, was much easier than the general college. It wasn't until the 1920s, when Babe Ruth propelled professional baseball to the forefront of the national consciousness, that colleges began to question the use of professional players.

"I'm not only saying it is right for a man to play summer baseball for money, but I am going further than that," said Clarkson College president G. Stanley Hall. "He is failing in his duty to himself and to the world if he does not take advantage of his God-given talent to use it to the best of his ability."

FOOTBALL

The first intercollegiate football game was played on November 6, 1869. Rutgers beat Princeton, 6 to 4. There were ten freshmen on the Rutgers squad, three of whom were flunking algebra. Unlike the uncontrolled chaos that was Bloody Monday on the Harvard quad, in this game each team was limited to twenty-five players.

Three years later, Harvard played McGill University in a game that marked the first time that college sports teams wore uniforms. The Harvard players wore bandanas and sweaters in the school colors. McGill wore white duck trousers that eventually morphed into knee-length football pants, and turbans that eventually became helmets. In the latter half of the century, football began to spread to the Midwest. In 1879, the University of Michigan beat Racine (later the University of Wisconsin), 1 to 0.

Although there were a few programs sprinkled across the country, in the late 19th century football was very much an eastern sport. That's because Walter Chauncey Camp took the game that was a cross between soccer and rugby and made it the American football that we know today. Known as the "Father of American Football," Camp played football for Yale from 1877 through 1882. He was team captain in 1878, 1879, and 1881. He played four years as an undergraduate student and two years while in medical school, before becoming Yale's first head football coach, a position he held until 1910. Along the way, he introduced two of the most significant developments in the evolution of American football: the line of scrimmage and the down system.

Before Camp came along, football was very much like rugby, with play centered around a scrum, in which each team fought for possession of the ball. Camp's line of scrimmage not only made play more orderly but also gave possession of the ball to one team, thus creating offense and defense. He also created the down system, which initially consisted of three chances to move the ball five yards. If the team with the ball failed, the other team took over. There were no punts.

With these new rules came new strategies. Teams developed specialized positions and plays that were integral to moving the ball downfield. The most deadly was the flying wedge, which was developed by Boston businessman Lorin F. Deland and was just as it sounds. The offensive line would lock arms and form a wedge, knocking down and stepping over anyone who got in its way. The flying wedge was basically an adaptation of the Napoleonic military strategy of concentrating force to pummel an enemy into submission. It worked almost as effectively on the football field as it did on the battlefield. In 1894, the *Boston Globe* reported twelve college football deaths, up from seven the year before, many of them attributed to the use of the flying wedge.

Despite this deadly turn in tactics, football continued to grow in popularity. By the mid-1890s, more than 120 schools had football teams. But Camp set a won-loss record that stands to this day. From 1875 to 1909, Yale's football team had an incredible record of 280-14. The 1888 team under Camp scored 698 points and shut out every opponent.

The one thing that kept college football from growing into the nationwide sport we know today was the sheer size of the United States. Traveling across the country in the late 19th century—before college athletic teams had their own private jets—was no easy thing. When Michigan invited Cornell to Ann Arbor for a football game, Cornell president Andrew D. White said, "I will not permit thirty men to travel four hundred miles just to agitate a bag of wind."

In addition to travel restrictions, you have to remember that much of the U.S. population was still concentrated east of the Appalachians. Therefore, the biggest game of the year was typically an Ivy League match-up played on Thanksgiving Day at New York's Polo Grounds before forty thousand screaming fans. But as football grew in stature and popularity, teams began to build their own stadiums. In 1903, Harvard built a thirty-thousand-seat football stadium. Four years later, the Yale Bowl, which can hold a whopping eighty thousand fans, went up in New Haven. The stadium sold out for all six home games, and the school grossed $16,000, or more than $325,000 in 2008 dollars.

WINNING—AND MONEY—IS EVERYTHING

Almost as soon as schools started to build football stadiums and reap significant revenue from college football, some began to question it. Many wondered if such a brutal sport had a place on the college campus. In 1889, Harvard president Charles Eliot studied the relationship between grades and football. He found that freshman football players had nearly four times as many D's and F's as A's and B's as the average student. And the increasing number of deaths from the flying wedge and other brutal tactics brought even more scrutiny to the game. Politicians and college presidents called for a thorough investigation into the toll football was taking on college athletes and academics. The presidents of Harvard, Princeton, and Yale, the college football powerhouses of the day, quickly agreed to try to rein in football, but the fix was in before the committee held its first meeting. That's because Walter Camp was selected to head up the investigation.

Camp produced a report for all to read, but it only highlighted the benefits of college football. He purposely left out the fact that one in five players was permanently maimed from playing college football and that about twenty players a year were killed playing the game. Indeed, the *Boston Globe* estimated that from 1880 to 1905 there were 330 deaths and 1,149 serious injuries that were a direct result of college football. Camp's report was, in effect, a complete whitewash—and it went almost unchallenged. Indeed, none other than Senator Henry Cabot Lodge defended football as being an essential part of the collegiate experience.

"Winning in American college football meant the chance to prove something: virility, social worthiness or elitism," wrote Francis Dealy. "No other activity could counter the image of a bookish and effete college student better than football, a real man's sport. No other activity could bolster a nation's virility."

Some schools had modest success establishing faculty committees to oversee athletics. But they were the exception. These committees often were heavily influenced by the money, power, and esteem that athletic programs brought to a university—even at the turn of the 20th century. And more often than not, the committees set up to rein in athletics were populated by wealthy (and influential) alumni who were mostly sympathetic to athletics. Many times, faculty advisers were nothing more than a token presence on these committees.

A good example was Harvard's so-called Board of Overseers. In 1897, it tried for the third time in six years to ban football. In the end, influential alumni, including future president Teddy Roosevelt, saved the sport. At about the same time, Dartmouth alumni took over the faculty athletics commission and used their own money—for facilities, coaches, and payola—to transform Dartmouth from a perennial loser into a football powerhouse. Similarly, Yale had a secret, alumni-funded $100,000 slush fund for the football team. Some of the money was used by Walter Camp to send Yale football captain James Hogan on a two-week, all-expenses-paid trip to the Caribbean.

This type of corruption—and payola—was rampant throughout college athletics at the turn of the century. In 1896, Lafayette College recruited an all-star tackle named Fielding Yost (no relation). There was just one problem. He was already a student at West Virginia University. That didn't matter. Lafayette just needed him to enroll for one week, so that he could help them end Penn's thirty-six-game winning streak. He did just that, leading Lafayette to a 6 to 4 victory. After the game was over, Yost went back to Morgantown. Ironically, he went on to become one of the most legendary athletic directors of all time. He built Michigan into an NCAA powerhouse in the early 20th century. Today, the Michigan hockey team plays its games at the Yost Ice Arena. I'll bet few Wolverine fans know—or care—that he began his college career as a hired gun, all too willing to bend the rules.

As mentioned, Yale used its $100,000 slush fund to pay star players such as tackle James Hogan. His compensation package included free tuition, meals, a suite in Vanderbilt Hall, a monopoly on the sale of game score-cards, and a job with the American Tobacco Company. With the exception of the last two items, this sounds like a typical athletic scholarship today.

While many readers may be appalled that an institution of Yale's academic repute would have a football slush fund, it was simple economics. The Princeton-Yale game typically drew forty thousand fans and generated revenues of more than $25,000. Yale didn't see this as cheating but rather the cost of doing business.

And Yale wasn't alone. Again, college sports at the turn of the 20th century was dominated by the Ivy League. Princeton president Woodrow Wilson, who would go on to lead the United States to victory in World War I and found the League of Nations, said in 1890, "Princeton is noted in this wide world for three things: Football, baseball, and collegiate instruction."

While many college administrators became enthralled with the notoriety (and revenues) that came with big-time college athletics, others saw what it was doing to the credibility of some of the nation's most esteemed academic institutions.

"Colleges are presenting themselves to the public, educated and uneducated alike, as places of mere physical sport and not as educational training institutions," bemoaned Harvard president Charles Eliot.

When football coaches' salaries began to eclipse those of the leading professors, there were people who tried to reign in college athletics. But it was mostly a futile effort. In the 1880s, several Harvard committees—made up mostly of academics—tried to ban football altogether. While their cause was righteous, they were always defeated by the might of the alumni association. In 1895, the Big Ten voted to restrict the use of freshmen and graduate students. When the Ivy League failed to follow its reforms, and the Big Ten started to lose ground financially and competitively, it rescinded the rule. In short, the financial lure of athletics was too much for even the most principled institutions. It prompted Cornell (Iowa) College President W. F. King to correctly observe in 1893 that "The hot competition in these games stimulates certain unfortunate practices, such as the admission of professionals into college as nominal students at the expense of the team, tendencies to betting, the limitation of the benefits of the game to a very few persons, and with these the interest is too intense to be compatible with educational advantages."

THE REFORMERS LOSE

In 1905, President Teddy Roosevelt summoned the presidents of Harvard, Princeton, and Yale to the White House to discuss the brutality of college football (Roosevelt's son had recently broken his nose in a Harvard football game). He threatened to forever ban football if something wasn't done to remedy the situation. On Dec. 28, 1905, at a meeting hosted by New York University president Henry MacCracken, the Intercollegiate Athletic Association of the United States (IAAUS) was founded, with sixty-two member schools. It would later become the National Collegiate Athletic Association. But like so many reform efforts of the past, the NCAA was not the answer to the problems that plagued college athletics. If anything, it only made things worse. Yes, there were modest rules changes, but with the advent of the NCAA, college football went boom, not bust.

From 1920 to 1940, more than forty new large stadiums were built to accommodate rapidly growing attendance at college football games.

"Popularity and greater investments only made winning more important," wrote noted sports economist Andrew Zimbalist in his excellent book, *Unpaid Professionals: Commercialism and Conflict in Big-Time College Sports.* "Cheating and financial scandals abounded."

Indeed, if the 19th century was noted for its under-the-table payments to athletes and the sheer brutality of college football, the 20th century marked the beginning of the media's love affair with college sports. Viewed more harshly, it also marked the beginning of the lavish pro-sports coverage that dominates local and national newspapers today, taken to a high art form by the twenty-four-hour all-sports channels and magazines such as *Sports Illustrated,* which long ago abandoned any façade of journalistic objectivity (if there ever was such a thing).

The burgeoning corruption of college athletics was well documented in a 1929 report issued by the Carnegie Commission. According to the report, three quarters of the 112 programs that were studied were in violation of the NCAA rules and the principles of amateurism.

The primary problem, the Carnegie Commission concluded, was commercialization: "An interlocking network that included expanded press coverage, public interest, alumni involvement and recruiting abuses."

The damning report went on to say that the primary victim of the commercialization of college athletics was "the student-athlete in particular, the diminishing of educational and intellectual values in general. Also, students (including non-athletes) were the losers because they had been denied their rightful involvement in sports."

If this sounds familiar, you're not mistaken. The problem that plagued college athletics in the 1930s—namely the corruption of rampant commercialism—is what plagues it today. The only difference is that the money at risk today has grown exponentially from the 1930s. Whereas college sports revenues in the 1930s were measured in the tens of thousands, today they're measured in the hundreds of millions.

The net result—a thesis that will be repeated and defended throughout this book—is that there's much more at stake today. Therefore it has become all the more important for the NCAA and its member institutions to perpetuate the façade of amateurism that was a blatant lie at the turn of the 20th century, and doubly so today. Moreover, not only have the NCAA and its member schools done little to try to curb this culture of corruption that infects college athletics today, they can rightly be seen as vigorously advancing the college-athletics revenue model that's the driving force behind the corruption.

In 1931, University of Chicago president Robert Hutchins, long a critic of the NCAA and college athletics in general, nailed it when he wrote, "College is not a great athletic association and social club, in which provision is made, merely incidentally, for intellectual activity on the part of the physically and socially unfit. College is an association of scholars in which provision is made for the development of traits and powers which must be cultivated, in addition to those which are purely intellectual, if one is to become a well-balanced and useful member of any community."

In 1939, the University of Chicago dropped its football program. A few years later, the football locker room was converted into the secret laboratory that developed the atom bomb. C. W. Watson, a retired Army intelligence officer, former college history professor, and 1958 graduate of The Citadel, once said famously, "As I recall, the University of Chicago doesn't have a football team. They just have the Manhattan Project."

Indeed.

ABSOLUTE POWER CORRUPTS ABSOLUTELY

But as college football continued to grow, the abuses only got larger and more blatant. Not even the hardship of World War II could curtail it. In fact, the war was used as an excuse to expand—not curtail—cheating and rules violations. The military's demand for college-age players intensified the recruiting of top high school athletes—regardless of their academic records. Schools also relaxed substitution rules and, for the first time, many developed a platoon system in which players were designated offense or defense; they didn't play both sides of the ball. All of this prompted *New York Herald Tribune* sports editor Stanley Woodward to write in 1946, "When it comes to chicanery, double-dealing, and undercover work behind the scenes, big-time college football is in a class by itself."

"Should the Carnegie Foundation launch an investigation of college football right now," he continued, "the mild breaches of etiquette uncovered [in the 1929 report] would assume a remote innocence which would only cause snickers among the post-war pirates."

Not much has changed today. Despite round after round of reform aimed at curbing cheating and upholding academic standards, the NCAA has been the proverbial Dutch boy with his finger in the dike. In 1986, the NCAA introduced Proposition 48, which set minimum academic standards for college athletes. In short, the NCAA was policing the admissions process, in effect saying that it was no longer up to the institutions themselves to determine if a kid could be admitted or not. The measure drew loud protests from black coaches, especially basketball coaches John Thompson at Georgetown and John Chaney of Temple. They claimed that Proposition 48 was unfair to black athletes because ongoing institutional racial discrimination didn't guarantee black students the same elementary and secondary educational opportunities as their white counterparts. When Proposition 16 was introduced ten years later, they went ballistic, threatening to boycott games.

High school graduates who did not meet Proposition 16's requirements were precluded from participating in intercollegiate competition and often were denied athletic scholarships. To qualify for full eligibility, student-athletes had to have a 2.0 grade-point average (GPA) in thirteen approved academic "core" courses and an SAT score of 1010 or a combined ACT score of 86. But there was a fudge factor. Students with lower test scores could still qualify if they had higher core-course GPAs. The minimum test score for students with a GPA of 2.5 or higher was 820 SAT/68 ACT.

Thompson, Chaney, and others argued that the use of the SAT cut-off score also was racially biased because blacks failed to reach it in markedly higher proportions than whites. Thompson said poor minority kids were at a disadvantage because they had to take the "mainstream-oriented" SAT.

"Certain kids require individual assessment," he said, obviously referring to his starting five. "Some urban schools cater to poor kids, low-income kids, black and white. To put everybody on the same playing field is just crazy."

Chaney argued in a *New York Times* op-ed that Proposition 16 excluded kids who could make it in college with help. He offered one of his own players, Rasheed Brokenborough, as an example of a poor black kid raised on the wrong side of the tracks in Philadelphia who scored too low on the SAT to be even a partial qualifier.

"That meant we could not provide him with any scholarship money, much as he needed it, during his freshman year, and he had to accumulate 24 credits or face expulsion," Chaney wrote. "Rasheed was a serious student and finished his course work in four years plus summer school."

Brokenborough went on to teach in the Philadelphia schools, but was "deeply in debt," Chaney said. "He was punished for a crime he did not commit."

The NCAA developed new eligibility standards in 2002 that initially required high school students to successfully complete fourteen core courses in English, history, the sciences, and mathematics with at least a 2.0 grade-point average. In subsequent years, it increased to sixteen core courses. The NCAA also created the NCAA Initial-Eligibility Clearinghouse, which approved these high school core courses and test scores. In other words, if a kid didn't clear the Clearinghouse, he was ineligible to play, even if the school thought he was academically qualified.

The new standards also require that college freshmen complete twenty-four hours of course work and have at least a 1.8 grade-point average. In addition, they call for completion of 40, 60, and 80 percent of the requirements for a degree by the end of collegiate years two, three, and four.

In 2005, the NCAA also introduced a new formula for the Graduation Success Rate (GSR), which measures the percentage of student-athletes who graduate. The old measurement was unfair, schools argued, because they were penalized for students who left in good academic standing either to transfer to another school or go to the pros. The newest six-year rolling average adjusts for this. So when you see a school report its GSR in 2008, you're really seeing how successful they were at graduating student-athletes who were freshmen in 2002.

The latest measurement of an athlete's academic success is the Academic Progress Rate (APR). Introduced in 2004, it was, contrary to the GSR, designed to give a more real-time measurement of a student-athlete's academic progress. One point is awarded each term to each scholarship student-athlete who meets academic-eligibility standards and an additional point is awarded if they remain with the institution. A team's APR is the total points earned by the team at a given time divided by the total points possible. A cutoff score of 925 corresponds to an anticipated graduation rate of about 65 percent, according to the NCAA. Teams that fall below the cutoff score on a statistically significant basis are subject to instantaneous penalties that become increasingly harsher if a school doesn't improve the academic progress of its athletes. These least painful penalties started after two years' worth of data were collected and took effect the following academic year. Teams that habitually failed to meet the cutoff could be subject to historical penalties, which began to be assessed in the 2008–9 school year. Historical penalties may include additional scholarship reductions, recruiting restrictions, or being barred from postseason competition, including bowl games.

But on the eve of the implementation of the harsher penalties, guess what was the hottest topic of discussion at Street and Smith's *Sports Business Journal*'s Collegiate Athletics seminar in New York in December 2007? You guessed it: reforming APR.

Pushing hard against proposals to water down penalties for habitually underperforming athletes were people such as Dr. Nathan Tublitz. When Dr. Tublitz isn't teaching neurobiology at the University of Oregon, he's co-chairman of the Coalition on Intercollegiate Athletics, a group of fifty-six Division 1 faculty senates whose primary mission is to remind college presidents, athletic directors, and coaches that the kids at center court during March Madness are supposed to be students first and athletes second.

That's a quaint notion in an era when CBS is paying $6.1 billion for the broadcast rights to March Madness.

"The GSR and APR are, potentially, very effective tools to improve academic standards and to allow student-athletes to achieve their educational goals," Dr. Tublitz said. "The key, of course, is in the implementation and enforcement of penalties that follow from schools that don't meet the standards."

In short, Dr. Tublitz is concerned that the APR—like many of the rules that govern recruiting, scholarships, and eligibility—will become for schools just another game of "catch us if you can." Furthermore, he worries that as the APR's true consequences are realized, schools will lobby the NCAA to water it down or make exceptions.

"When the data came out [in 2007] and the trends were becoming clearer, the NCAA pointed out publicly that they were expecting 45 percent of basketball teams, 40 percent of football teams, and 35 percent of all teams in Division I to be penalized under APR," Dr. Tublitz said. "The question is whether the NCAA will penalize all those teams that do not meet minimum APR benchmarks."

On average, Division I schools in 2008 were graduating about 77 percent of their athletes, according to the NCAA. But the numbers ran the gamut. For instance, looking at the Associated Press Top 25 for the week of March 10, 2008, number one North Carolina graduated 86 percent of its basketball players using the NCAA's GSR measure, while number two Memphis graduated just 40 percent. Looking at the APR, the more real-time measure, North Carolina scored 993, well above the minimum requirement of 925. Memphis, by contrast, had an APR of just 916, which would result in penalties under the NCAA's new rules.

For its part, the NCAA insists that it's serious about enforcing the new standards, regardless of a team's national ranking.

"This is a real-time measure that has a component of accountability that's tied to consequences," said Kevin Lennon, the NCAA's vice president for membership services. "That's unique. We have not had this before."

Mr. Lennon also said that the new penalties would carry "a broader recognition" for teams that perform poorly in the classroom.

"We feel that under these new measures, they'll want to avoid being labeled as underperforming," he said. "And they want to avoid the penalties that will impact their ability to compete."

Dr. Tublitz concedes that there's only so much that the NCAA can do. The bigger problem is with a sports-mad American culture that doesn't care how college athletes are admitted, if they graduate, or if they ever make it to the NBA. All that most fans care about, he says, is winning championships—whatever the cost.

"You have to stop the drift away from academics, and our universities are the standard-bearers for maintaining academic standards," Dr. Tublitz said. "Thus it seems appropriate for our universities to be the first in line to say we should reverse this cultural trend and not continue to look the other way when students are accepted primarily for their athletic prowess."

More important, schools aren't doing these kids any favors by admitting them when it's unlikely that they will succeed academically.

"We bring in seventeen-year-old kids, some of them from the inner city," Tublitz said. "We wine and dine them. They have female chaperones. We put them up in fancy hotels. They come here and see an incredibly fancy locker room with individual TV screens, air conditioning, and videogames. They go in and see the new football stadium and the new $200 million basketball arena. They see a medical training facility that is stunningly beautiful with waterfalls, treadmill pools, and state-of-the-art medical and dental equipment.

"They come here and are treated like royalty," he continued. "Until they break a leg or get put on the second string and then they get set aside. Many don't earn a degree. They don't have the training or the skills to be independent after they leave the university. They're lost."

Indeed, only about 3 percent of high school basketball players will get a Division I scholarship. And less than 2 percent of those who do will have a meaningful NBA career.

"What about the 97 percent?" Dr. Tublitz asks. "We need to give them the tools to succeed beyond athletics, and we're not doing that."

And, of course, many of these kids are African-Americans from poor social circumstances.

"It's no coincidence that basketball has the lowest APR," Dr. Tublitz said. "One of the major determinants of college success is socioeconomic status. Kids from privileged backgrounds, on average, do better. As educators, we need to make sure that those kids from underprivileged backgrounds are given the skills to achieve their potential. We need to put more resources into that group of students."

In fact, the trend is just the opposite. According to a report last year in the *Journal of Sports Management,* alumni giving at the nation's one hundred biggest athletic departments was up significantly, while academic giving at the same schools remained flat. That's a significant shift. In 1998, athletics gifts accounted for 14.7 percent of all donations. By 2003, the figure had increased to 26 percent.

With these increased donations, often comes increased pressure to win.

"There's a correlation between Oregon's attempt to have winning teams and the quality of students that they have to attract in order to achieve that goal," Dr. Tublitz said of his own campus. "This is not rocket science. It's not neuroscience. There are many extremely talented athletes for whom academics is not their primary goal at university. The fact that many people are OK with that says a lot about who we are and what we value."

3 WHO'S REALLY
THE BCS CHAMPION?

There are no better examples of how billion-dollar sponsorships and media rights contracts have had an impact on college athletics than college football's bowl system and college basketball's March Madness. And here's why: winning records don't have a direct impact on alumni giving, but success in postseason play does.

Those are the findings of sports economists Robert Baade and Jeffrey Sundberg of Lake Forest (Illinois) College in their study, "What Determines Alumni Generosity?" They looked at public and private colleges, tried to compensate for other mitigating factors, and came to the conclusion that "in the doctorate-granting institutions success as measured by a postseason football bowl game translates into higher giving. NCAA men's basketball tournament appearances are correlated with higher alumni giving at public universities, but not private. At liberal arts colleges, athletic success as measured by winning percentage has a statistically significant, but small, effect on alumni giving."

They found that alumni giving for a successful college bowl game increased on average by about 54 percent.

"Given an average giving level of $75 per alum, this amounts to about $40 per alum," they learned. "The average total alumni giving in the private university sample is roughly $4.3 million, so that a bowl appearance can be expected to increase alumni giving by over $2 million for an institution of average size. An appearance in the NCAA basketball tournament is not correlated with increases in the average gift."

For a public university, the impact is significantly smaller, estimated at about $500,000 on average, according to the authors. And unlike private universities, public universities do see a positive impact on alumni giving from the NCAA basketball tournament.

"The predicted increase in alumni giving for an institution of average size is just over $450,000, an increase of 35 percent," the authors said.

The authors concluded, "In both the public and private university samples, winning percentages were not a significant determinant of alumni giving, yet bowl appearances were significant in both, as were basketball tournament appearances in the public sample."

In short, a bowl game or NCAA tourney appearance legitimizes a good season, while a good season without postseason play is a disappointment for many boosters.

"In the end, a football record of 7-4 with a subsequent bowl appearance is more satisfying (and gives the university more publicity) than a record of 8-3 without a bowl bid, a conclusion with which most fans will agree."

Although the study was groundbreaking in its research and conclusions, I think it's fair to say that Baade and Sundberg only verified quantitatively what the general public has instinctively known for a long time, namely, that college bowl games can be very lucrative for participating schools. But who are the big winners when it comes to the economics of today's college football bowl games and basketball's March Madness? The answer will surprise you. But first, a little history.

THE NAME GAME

When did Corporate America discover college bowl games and turn these venerable New Year's Day traditions into crass commercial messages with tongue-twisting names? It was 1986, to be exact. That's when the Sun Bowl Association signed a five-year sponsorship agreement with John Hancock Financial Services, making the bowl the John Hancock Sun Bowl. Two years later, the Sun Bowl made its first-ever $1 million payment to the competing teams, Alabama and Army.

Media rights have grown over the years, as well. In 2001, the Sun Bowl committee signed its first-ever six-year television extension with CBS

Sports, valued at about $1 million. The current broadcast contract runs through 2009.

The CBS renewal in 2001 allowed the Sun Bowl Association to undertake a massive renovation of the University of Texas–El Paso stadium where the game is played each year. It included a new field made of AstroPlay and a Diamond Vision big-screen scoreboard.

Today, the game is known as the Brut Sun Bowl, the eighth name change in its seventy-five-year history (second in longevity only to the Rose Bowl). In years past, it had been known as the John Hancock Sun Bowl (1986–89), the John Hancock Bowl (1990–93), the Norwest Sun Bowl (1996–98), the Wells Fargo Sun Bowl (1999–2003), and the Vitalis Sun Bowl (2004–7). There was a sponsorship hiatus in 1994–95.

While it's hard to keep track of the name, it's not hard to keep track of the money. In 2005, the Sun Bowl paid $1.5 million to each participating team. In 2008, the game was a dud, as Oregon State beat Pittsburgh 3 to 0, but the payout had risen to $1.9 million for each team.

Once John Hancock opened the floodgates in 1986, it was just a few years before every bowl game started selling naming rights and cashing in. That's how we got to the corporate-inspired beauties that we have today, including the San Diego County Credit Union Poinsettia Bowl, the Meineke Car Care Bowl, the Bell Helicopter Armed Forces Bowl, and the Rose Bowl Presented by Citi. As annoying as these corporate names may be, it's hard to argue with the economics of today's bowl games.

For a long time, there were just four important bowl games: the Cotton Bowl, the Orange Bowl, the Sugar Bowl, and "the granddaddy of them all," the Rose Bowl. The number of postseason bowl games has grown to thirty-four in 2009, and most are multimillion-dollar enterprises, but the bowl games had much more humble beginnings. Originally, they were merely a showcase for their sun-drenched host city, hoping to lure tourists and the fans of the football-mad conferences that anchored the bowls. The Cotton Bowl in Dallas traditionally featured a Southwest Conference team, usually Arkansas or Texas; in Miami, the Orange Bowl always had an ACC team; the Sugar Bowl in New Orleans was anchored by the SEC (often Alabama); and the Rose Bowl always featured a match-up between one of the best PAC-10 teams—usually USC or Stanford—against one of the country's top-ranked teams. The Big Ten eventually became the opponent of choice in the Rose Bowl, mainly because Michigan, Ohio State, and Wisconsin consistently produced winning teams and drew thousands of boosters already tired of winter to the warm climate of Southern California.

Although there were thirty-four major and minor bowl games in 2009, only five make up the Bowl Championship Series: the Fiesta, Orange, Rose, and Sugar bowls, along with the BCS Championship game, which features what organizers believe to be the two best teams in the country. In 2009, those were Florida and Oklahoma. The Gators defeated the Sooners, 24 to 14.

These five premier bowl games generate more than $100 million in revenue. In 2006, the BCS divided $89 million between the six participants in the Tostitos Fiesta Bowl, the FedEx Orange Bowl, and the Nokia Sugar Bowl. (Teams in the Rose Bowl and BCS Championship game are paid separately.)

Most conferences have some sort of revenue sharing, so that means that every time Michigan, Ohio State, or Wisconsin goes to a bowl game, they split the money equally (after expenses) with the other ten members of the Big Ten, including perpetual also-rans Minnesota, Northwestern, and Indiana. What many people don't know is that while the teams do well in racking up postseason bowl money, the real winners are the privately held bowl committees, which operate like charities. And there's perhaps no better example of how these once-quaint New Year's Day traditions have morphed into multimillion-dollar moneymaking machines than the Chick-fil-A (formerly Peach) Bowl.

The latest name change took place after the 2005 game with an added million bucks from title sponsor Chick-fil-A, a fast-food restaurant based in the Southeast whose ads entice diners away from McDonald's and Burger King with a herd of mischievous animated cows whose mantra is, "Eat Mor Chikin." It's been a partnership that has paid huge dividends.

When the bowl began, instead of playing outdoors in the now-defunct Fulton County Stadium, the game moved indoors to the Georgia Dome, which has been upgraded with luxury suites, a club level, and an A-list private dining room thanks to Arthur Blank, the archetype for the business-savvy 21st-century NFL franchise owner, whose Atlanta Falcons play there the rest of the year. In 2009, the SEC's LSU Tigers beat the ACC's Georgia Tech Yellow Jackets, 38 to 3. The game was the bowl's twelfth-straight sell-out, generating about $12 million in revenues, offset by expenses of about $10 million, resulting in a roughly $2 million profit. The bowl has seen revenues climb more than 70 percent over the past six years, a marked improvement from the dark days of the 1980s and 1990s when the bowl actually lost money. Thanks to these newfound riches, the Chick-fil-A Bowl was the most profitable non-BCS bowl game in 2008, according to Street & Smith's *Sports Business Journal.*

"Most bowl presidents/chairmen make more than $200,000 a year and some collect nearly $500,000 annually," SBJ said in its December 2007 profile of the major bowl games. "The top two executives at the Fiesta Bowl were paid a total of $770,000, according to the bowl's 2005 Form 990, the tax return used by nonprofit groups. The Outback Bowl spent over $1 million in salary and benefits for its top five executives, and its CEO, Jim McVay, makes $498,000 a year, putting him at the top of the salary chart."

The bowl committees can afford to pay those salaries. Revenues for the twenty-two postseason bowl games range from $1.3 million for the R&L Carriers New Orleans Bowl to more than $16 million for some of the top BCS events. And that doesn't include television rights and sponsorship revenue, which go to the bowl committees, not the conferences. When you factor those monies in, revenue from the Orange, Sugar, Rose, and Fiesta bowls is estimated at well over $30 million a year—each. Add those numbers in with the bowls that don't file tax returns as nonprofits and the thirty-four postseason college bowl games are a $400-million-a-year industry.

"The whole model of doing business has changed," said Keith Tribble, former athletic director at the University of Central Florida and CEO of the Orange Bowl until 2006. During his thirteen-year tenure, bowl revenue increased from $8 million to more than $30 million.

"We ran it like a business, like a major corporation," he told *Sports Business Journal.* "That's how we found the dollar value in it."

"The bowls aren't bowls, they're commercial enterprises," said Charles Young, the former chancellor of UCLA and the president of the University of Florida, told the *Arizona Republic.* "The game used to help pay for a parade and other activities. The bowl chairmen were volunteers. Now the bowls are serving too many masters."

The most important masters, of course, are the participating schools themselves, which rely on postseason bowl money to keep their athletic departments in the black. And it's not just the top-tier bowls but also the lesser ones, such as the Motor City and Meineke Car Care Bowls, that are being driven hard to generate more revenues.

"Everybody needs the revenue to stay competitive," Tribble said.

And they seem to be getting it.

Chick-fil-A Bowl

Under terms of its new contract, Chick-fil-A is paying $22 million over five years for its title sponsorship of the game formerly known as the Peach Bowl. In 2006, the bowl's media revenue from ESPN doubled from $1.3 million to $2.6 million, part of a deal in which Chick-fil-A also agreed to buy airtime on the cable sports network throughout the college football season. Simply raising ticket prices by $5 brought in another $400,000.

Those are the three T's of bowl revenue: tickets, TV, and title.

Conference revenue sharing notwithstanding, the schools make out pretty well, too (Table 3.1). The Chick-fil-A Bowl pays $5.6 million: $3.3 million to the ACC team and $2.4 million to the SEC squad. The Capital One Bowl is the top-paying non-BCS bowl, with a payout of $8.5 million (on revenue of $13.5 million). The Cotton and Outback bowls each pay $6 million. By comparison, the BCS bowls pay about $17 million per team.

The Chick-fil-A Bowl also donates more than $1 million to local charities, which in turn has lured valuable sponsorship money from Atlanta-based businesses such as Coca-Cola and Delta Airlines. That's how the bowl turned its nearly $2 million profit.

Most important for Chick-fil-A, which is largely credited with helping to turn around the bowl's finances, the sponsorship money isn't just a tax write-off. It pays dividends well beyond the bowl game itself.

"The college audience tends to be a higher-income audience, they index higher on retail, they index higher as a casual-food diner, and we know

TABLE 3.1
Chick-fil-A Bowl Key Revenue and Expenses

Revenue		Expenses	
Ticket sales	$4.2M	Team payouts	$5.6M
Media rights	$2.6M	NCAA certification	$12,000
Sponsorships	Close to $4M	Management fee	$308,367[a]
Memberships	$841,543	Branding	$2.9M[b]
Merchandise	$83,100		

Source: Street & Smith's *Sports Business Journal.*
[a]Paid to Metro Atlanta Chamber of Commerce.
[b]Cost to change name from Chick-fil-A Peach Bowl to simply Chick-fil-A Bowl.

they're very loyal to their college brand, so that rubs off on the brands that partner with their schools," Steve Robinson, senior vice president of marketing for Chick-fil-A, told *Sports Business Journal.*

Adding further to the positive economics for Chick-fil-A is the fact that about 60 percent of its restaurants are within the footprint of the SEC and ACC. That led to Chick-fil-A also becoming a corporate partner of the ACC, SEC, and Big 12 conferences.

"We can't afford to do everything, so we've just decided to focus on the collegiate fan and support their schools," Robinson said.

Other bowl games do equally well. The Allstate Sugar Bowl brings in revenue of nearly $11 million, the Gator Bowl $14 million, the Orange Bowl $16 million. Even some of the smaller, more obscure bowl games do well financially. The Pacific Life Holiday Bowl generates revenues of nearly $10 million. The Petro Sun Independence Bowl brings in $3 million. The Music City Bowl generates more than $3 million, and the Roady's Humanitarian Bowl $1.6 million. The Rose Bowl has long been called "the granddaddy of them all" (a phrase coined by ABC college football broadcaster Keith Jackson), but it isn't anymore.

The Rose Bowl generates $4.6 million from game-day revenue, $1.3 million from licensing, $355,000 from sponsorships, $722,000 from travel and tourism, and slightly more than $1 million in ticket sales. It also gets $61,000 from concessions commissions and $22,000 in local government aid. The Rose Bowl's total receipts are a little more than $12 million. Among its expenses is $950,000 to lease the Rose Bowl itself, $635,000 to the City of

Pasadena, $300,000 for marketing and promotions, and $450,000 in comp tickets for VIPs. But by far the biggest expense is salaries, which come in at a whopping $1.7 million. CEO John M. Dorger is paid more than $250,000; COO William B. Flinn $138,000; CFO Jeffrey J. Allen $120,000; and Amy Wischnia, director of game operations, $100,000.

They're not alone. Most bowl executives are paid six-figure salaries. According to 2006 tax returns, the Sugar Bowl's Paul Hoolahan makes at least $462,000 a year and the Outback Bowl's Jim McVay $490,000, while the Gator Bowl's Rick Catlett receives more than $283,000 in salary and $55,000 in other compensation and benefits. Chick-fil-A Bowl director Gary Stokan is paid over $258,000, while board member Sam Williams is paid a whopping $638,000.

Even the players do well. While parents were scrambling in store aisles during the 2007 Christmas holiday season to find the Nintendo Wii, players in the Pacific Life Holiday Bowl were each given one of the game systems, which retail for $249, along with the Madden NFL 08 game. Players in the San Diego Credit Union Poinsettia Bowl got a copy of Madden NFL 08 as well, along with a Sony PSP Slim to play it on. For appearing in the BCS Championship game, players from Ohio State and LSU each received a Wii, Madden NFL 08, and two other games.

The most ironic gift of the 2008 bowl season was given out by the Gaylord Hotels Music City Bowl, which featured Florida State and Kentucky. Florida State showed up twenty players short, all of whom were suspended for cheating on an open-book music test. Too bad, because they missed out on a Sirius Satellite Radio unit, with was given to Music City Bowl players, along with a year's free subscription.

(I wonder if the players who didn't make it to the game got one anyway, since anyone who has to cheat on an open-book music test is certainly in need of all the music education they can get.)

And 2009 added a new wrinkle to the bowl gift-giving bonanza. Sony actually set up a suite in the hotels where the players for both the BCS and Orange Bowl were staying. In keeping within the NCAA's $750 restriction on postseason gift-giving, players were allowed to stroll the Sony Suite and, with $300 credit, pick a variety of items, including PlayStations and thirteen-inch flat-screen TVs. Sony would even ship the goods for the players. In addition to player gifts, schools often buy bowl game gift bags for the high-roller alumni and other VIPs they bring to the game. In fact, in 2009, Sony said it had five hundred extra gift bags made up with items stamped with the bowl logos, confident that schools would snatch them up.

The Rose Bowl

Although it may not be "the granddaddy of them all" anymore, the Rose Bowl is still a pretty big deal. While the numbers are certainly inflated, the UCLA Anderson School estimated that the Rose Bowl generates more than $200 million in direct and $370 million in indirect economic impact on the Southern California economy. That, of course, includes the Rose Bowl Parade, which kicks off the day at 8:00 A.M. The 2008 Rose Bowl featured USC, playing in what was essentially a home game, against the Big Ten's University of Illinois. Celebrity chef Emeril Lagasse was the grand marshal; the U.S. Navy SEAL's Leap Frogs parachute team delivered the coin to midfield that would be used for the coin toss. And, of course, both the USC and Illinois marching bands were there, performing both before the game and at halftime. The game, unfortunately, was a snoozer, with USC drubbing Illinois 41 to 10. In 2009, it was another USC victory, this time over Joe Paterno's Penn State.

But it wasn't the quality of play that was generating controversy for the bowl games in 2008, it was the paydays. In short, many people feel that the bowls have become too rich and too powerful.

"The bowls have become this big gravy train," said Murray Sperber, author of *College Sports Inc.*, a critical look at the business of college athletics. "Everybody loves this gravy train so much they don't want to get off. It's really one of the most corrupt boondoggles in college and university life."

NOT A PERFECT SYSTEM

Sperber is not alone. Many people are critical of the current system. For instance, between 2001 and 2005, seven tax-exempt bowls received $21.6 million in government aid. The Sugar Bowl, which in one four-year period received $4.1 million in funding from the Louisiana Department of Economic Development, pays a consultant $11,000 a year to "monitor legislative developments . . . related to the continued financial support of the Sugar Bowl." From 2001 through 2005, 38 percent of the Sun Bowl's total revenue, or about $9 million, came from receipts from a state rental car tax that are diverted into the bowl's bank account.

Like any government revenue stream, the one flowing to the bowl committees is guarded by an army of high-paid lobbyists. For instance, the Washington, D.C., lobbying firm run by former University of Oklahoma quarterback and Congressman J. C. Watts has been paid more than $500,000 in consulting fees from the BCS, according to congressional filings. And, of course, the power and success of today's bowl system owes much to the federal government.

Most sports economists and academics cite two favorable rulings for the bowl committees. In 1984 the U.S. Supreme Court ruled that the NCAA's strict control of the television schedule was an antitrust violation. Then in 1991 the IRS audited the Cotton Bowl committee and ruled that a sponsorship deal it had with Mobil that included naming rights was advertising and, therefore, taxable. Fearing the end of their financial gravy train, the bowl committees reached out to their friends in Congress, which passed legislation in 1997 that allowed sponsorship payments to nonprofits to be tax-exempt.

"The IRS had its head handed to them," said Les Lenkowsky, director of the graduate program at Indiana University's Center on Philanthropy.

Since the favorable IRS ruling on their tax-exempt status and sponsorships, the number of bowls has grown from eighteen in 1996 to thirty-four in 2009. With the protection of the federal government, some bowl committee members and school officials aren't ashamed of the piles of money that these bowls generate every year.

"Bowls have always been commercial ventures by nature," former Pac-10 commissioner Tom Hansen told the *Orange County Register* candidly in a December 2007 interview. "They really don't care about how good you are but about how many people you can bring."

"We do these games to generate economic impact," Bruce Binkowski, executive director of San Diego's Holiday and Poinsettia bowls, said in the same *Orange County Register* story. "To get people into town during a slow time of year."

While everyone knows the bowls are hugely profitable moneymaking ventures, IRS rules require the bowl committees to defend their tax-exempt status every few years. Some of the answers are hilarious (and incredulous).

"The organization conducts the Fed-Ex Orange Bowl so that residents and visitors of the community become interested in the climatic, recreational, commercial, agricultural, social, educational, and economic interests of the area," said the Orange Bowl in its fiscal 2005 filing. In the same filing, it reported $22.6 million in gross receipts.

"The notion that the stated pretext has anything to do with the reality is absurd," said sports economist Andrew Zimbalist.

And if you're wondering about the sky-high salaries of the bowl committee executives, that's covered by IRS regulations as well. According to the agency that every American loves to hate, even nonprofits can pay market-scale wages to their executives. Which brings us back to the Tostitos Fiesta Bowl.

John Junker is director of both the Fiesta and Insight.com bowls. In 2005, he received total compensation of $415,000. According to IRS filings, Junker worked thirty-one hours per week in 2005 for Arizona Sports, the primary Fiesta Bowl group, and was paid $264,500. He worked twenty-four hours a week for Fiesta Events, the nonprofit organization that handles Fiesta Bowl–related activities, and was paid $91,300. He spent another fifteen hours per week working for the Sun Bowl Foundation, which runs the Insight.com Bowl, and was paid $59,100. The Arizona Sports Foundation also gave Junker a $100,000 interest-free loan. Between 2001 and 2005, the two bowls that Junker oversees generated more than $110 million in gross receipts.

"I don't think my compensation is anybody's business other than myself and my board of directors," Junker told the *Arizona Republic*. "I work hard and I'm also not a believer in socialism, and socialism is what some of these people who are against the bowls want. And socialism has been one of the biggest purveyors of pain and deprivation throughout history."

OK. I guess that settles that. But others disagree.

"The current bowl system needs overhauling," former NCAA executive director Cedric Dempsey told the *Arizona Republic*. "But the people that control college football don't want to give up that control, control of all that money."

And they use that money to maintain that control. In addition to lobbying state and federal government, bowl directors spend hundreds of thousands of dollars a year traveling to games to schmooze coaches, athletic directors, college presidents, and conference commissioners.

"Because of the relationships the bowls have with the schools, the conferences, the bowls make sure they take care of everybody and everybody scratches each other's backs," said Zimbalist. "College presidents get wined and dined by the bowls. Deans, trustees are taken out by the bowls for a round of golf."

In 2005, the Orange Bowl spent $450,459 on travel, part of it obviously used to nurture important business relationships. The Outback Bowl has spent $3.5 million on social functions since 2001. And the Chick-fil-A Bowl has spent more than $4 million on business and marketing conferences since 2001.

"It's a good old boys' club," said Zimbalist. "Everybody gets treated royally well."

That's unlikely to change anytime soon.

A TRUE NATIONAL CHAMPION?

While few were fretting over what some see as the economic inequities of the current college football bowl system, the issue that was getting the most traction in 2009 was the clamor for a true "national championship" game that would settle once and for all who was the best college football team in the country. But in 2009, even that seemed to be a nonstarter.

Academics and administrators argue that an added bowl game beyond the current slate of New Year's games would run too far into the semester, disrupting the academic schedules of these players who are supposed to be students first and athletes second. And although the NCAA has little control over the BCS—and only sees $12,000 in consulting fees from each game—it would have to authorize another game.

Schools "would probably vote for it with some reluctance," said NCAA president Myles Brand. "And I probably would, too."

"I have some concerns about the academic side," he said. "But two teams? I don't think that's overwhelming."

Officials in most of the conferences that participate in the Bowl Championship Series are interested in exploring an added game that would determine a national champion. In one proposed formula, BCS rankings would be recalculated after the bowl games, and whoever is ranked number one and number two would play in the title game, with the winner able to claim that they were "the national champion." In another proposed playoff system, the BCS would seed the top four teams and stage what would amount to semifinals in two of its bowls. The winners would then play for the title.

As much as fans would like to see a true college playoff system that culminates with the crowning of a national champion, many think it will have to wait until at least 2013. The current BCS television contract expires after the 2009 season, but the Big Ten and Pac-10 broadcast contracts don't expire until 2012.

"Certainly, the media is unhappy and a number of the avid fans are unhappy, and they express it," Brand said. "But their unhappiness is not translating to a lack of interest. So I don't think it's as major a problem as some people think it is."

"I don't know who the BCS benefits," said Paul Happe, a Notre Dame alumnus and frequent commentator on the NDNation Web site. "It only works when two teams are clearly superior to all the other contenders. That happens occasionally, most recently in 2005. Most years there are four or five teams that could make a reasonable argument that they could win, if given a title shot. Yet in 2007, the BCS used a suspect 'formula' to pick Ohio State, a team that feasted on a schedule of cupcakes to face a Louisiana State team with two losses."

Happe went on to note that while Ohio State and LSU were certainly national championship contenders, so, too, were Southern Cal, Missouri, Georgia, Kansas, and West Virginia.

"Why not settle it on the field?" he said. "Who benefits from the BCS? Certainly not the fans. The BCS routinely engineers blowouts, in the title game and in all the other bowls that it represents. A playoff would have blowouts too, but you would know that the winner faced a more worthy opponent in the next round and that the champion would deserve the title."

Moreover, Happe said, the fans clearly want a playoff. As already noted, the argument against it is that an extra week or two of games in January would take the players away from the start of the spring semester.

"LSU and Ohio State boast minority graduation rates of 37 percent and 32 percent, respectively," Happe pointed out, citing statistics that are compiled by *Boston Globe* columnist Derrick Jackson every year. "I'm sure both institutions are real serious about their scholar-athletes."

Happe also noted that the NCAA had changed its rules to allow all teams to play a twelfth regular-season game, proving that their rhetoric is empty.

A true college playoff system may have to wait, but the more heated debate on the NDNation blog in 2008 was the economics of the school's recently renegotiated BCS contract. Although other bowl teams have to share revenue within their conference, Notre Dame, which is an independent and has one of the biggest college football fan bases in the country, has its own deal. In 2006, Notre Dame received $14.5 million for appearing in the Fiesta Bowl. Earlier, Notre Dame had renegotiated its BCS contract, which kicked in during the 2007 season. Under the deal, Notre Dame's share of any bowl money is just $4.5 million in years that it participates in the BCS. In those years that it doesn't get a BCS bowl bid, such as 2007–8, when the team went an abysmal 3-9, they get a guaranteed $1.3 million (on top of what they'd get if they went to a non-BCS bowl). Under the previous contract, Notre Dame received no money if it didn't play in a BCS game. So in essence, Notre Dame is guaranteed $1.3 million a year from the BCS, regardless of how well the team does.

When the contract was first renegotiated, many Notre Dame fans were furious, as evidenced by the chatter on the NDNation blog.

"The BCS renegotiated its contract with Notre Dame at the worst possible time for the Irish, when the program was down and BCS eligibility looked a long way off," said Happe. "They offered a tiny amount of guaranteed money, in exchange for gutting the big paydays that were sure to follow once the program was put back on solid footing. Our athletic director didn't have enough faith and took the sure money.

"College programs, especially one as legendary as Notre Dame, can rebuild quickly," he continued. "Sure enough, the team was back in the BCS even before the new contract went into effect. Two years into the new contract, we're nearly $8 million down."

In short, it's all about the money.

ESPN CROWNS A HIGH SCHOOL CHAMPION

While the college ranks have to wait for a change in the BCS system to crown a national championship, that's not a problem in high school football. On January 5, 2007, ESPN broadcast the first-ever Under Armour High School All-American Game from Orlando, Florida. With all the hype, fanfare, and sponsorship of a college bowl game, this game featured the top eighty high school football players in the country. And it's just another example of how the big bucks of college athletics are influencing the players—and economics—of the high school and prep ranks.

Under Armour, like every sports apparel maker and shoe company, is no stranger to trolling the elite ranks of high school and prep sports to find the next O. J. Mayo and Reggie Bush—and make sure they have plenty of free swag. Under Armour has been the title sponsor of ESPN's All-America Lacrosse Classic for the past two years and sees the football sponsorship as an extension of that program.

"Football was the sport our brand was built around," Steve Battista, vice president of brand for Under Armour, told *Sports Business Journal.* "This is the cornerstone of the entire suite of all-American games we're building out."

The game is the fourth elite high school sports event that Under Armour sponsors. It also has primary naming rights for national high school championships in baseball and softball in addition to lacrosse and football.

Battista said Under Armour hoped to add a fifth high school championship game in 2008.

Although high school players are as prohibited as their college heroes from taking sponsorship and endorsement money from agents and apparel companies, the all-American football game is a joint effort between ESPN and Intersport, a Chicago-based sports marketing company. The game is the culmination of ESPN's season-long effort to air live high school football games on its newest channel, ESPNU.

High school players are forbidden by NCAA regulations from talking to sports agents, but they're selected on the basis of analysis by ESPN Scouts Inc. And while NCAA regulations strictly regulate when and where college coaches can watch prospective recruits practice and are forbidden from putting them through tryout drills, there was also a skills competition that was televised on ESPN2 on January 4, 2008. Burger King was the title sponsor of the skills competition. The U.S. Marine Corps is a supporting sponsor for the game.

In short, not only has big money infected the college bowl system, it's snaked its way down to the high school and prep ranks, as well. But if you think the bowl games are awash in cash, they're nothing compared with the annual sports frenzy known as March Madness.

4 MONEY MADNESS

When it comes to pure money and brand awareness, March Madness, the month-long basketball bacchanalia that occurs each spring, dwarfs everything except the Super Bowl. The CBS television contract is worth $6.1 billion—yes, that's with a *b*. How does CBS justify that expense? Easy.

According to Dow Jones Newswires, CBS's second-quarter net income dropped 48 percent when the basketball tournament's schedule put some of the March Madness advertising revenue into CBS's first-quarter reporting period instead of the second. Further validating the tourney's popularity and drawing power is the fact that Americans participating in betting pools and watching games over the Internet cost employers an estimated $4 billion (that's also with a *b*) in lost productivity each March.

For the teams, the annual college basketball tournament is their chance to shine. For their schools, it's a chance to rack up huge merchandise sales and rake in big tournament payouts. Like Kansas State and its hiring of Bob Huggins, an NCAA Final Four appearance can take a heretofore unknown little school and turn it into a national brand.

Indeed, walk into a Lids cap store in a suburban shopping mall in Minneapolis—or most anywhere—and in addition to hats for Minnesota, Wisconsin, Iowa, or whomever the local university, you'll see merchandise for Duke, Georgia, Florida State, and North Carolina. These schools don't play their regular games anywhere near the retail outlet. But thanks to March Madness they have such far-reaching national brand awareness that a store in a state more well-known for hockey than basketball stocks their merchandise. And like many other aspects of college athletics, the revenues from these merchandise sales don't just go to the jocks.

University of North Carolina Tar Heel merchandise brings in about $6 million a year in trademark royalties for the Chapel Hill, North Carolina, school. Only 25 percent of that money goes to the athletic department; the remaining 75 percent is used for academic scholarships and need-based financial aid, which funds more than two thousand full-time students.

"Big wins mean big money," said Rutledge Tufts Jr., a director at Collegiate Licensing Corp., the Atlanta-based company that manages branding and merchandising for the NCAA, as well as many colleges and universities.

So as North Carolina's basketball program has stacked up national championships, the school has also stacked up piles of money from nationwide merchandise sales.

High-profile teams, tournament appearances, and lucrative television contracts bring in corporate sponsors, too. Ad spending during 2008 March Madness was estimated to be $545 million. From 1998 through 2007, television ad spending during the tournament was estimated at $3.8 billion, from over three hundred different advertisers. Cingular Wireless, Coca-Cola, General Motors, and others paid $35 million each to be signature sponsors of the 2008 event. Smaller sponsorships with Kraft and The Hartford Financial Group bring in $5 million to $10 million each.

AT&T, which sponsored the Final Four halftime show, was the big winner in 2007. The company formerly known as "Ma Bell" garnered an estimated 263 million "brand impressions" during the CBS television broadcast, according to A. C. Nielsen. The telecom giant also got 13 million "image-based impressions" on CBSSportsLine.com, which broadcasts the games over the Internet. General Motors, whose now-defunct Pontiac division sponsored the 2007 pregame show, came in second with 226 million impressions on television, but was the big winner online with 30 million hits. According to Street & Smith's *Sports Business Journal*, "AT&T augmented its TV exposure with sponsorship of March Madness on Demand, where tournament games were streamed live. It's likely that many viewers were multitasking and watching games on both TV and the Web simultaneously, giving AT&T a sort of dual, same-time exposure."

"More and more people are going to the Web for sports content, raising advertisers' confidence in their online sponsorships," said Michael Pond, a media analyst for Nielsen/NetRatings.

And while storied programs such as Kentucky, North Carolina, and Arizona can count on huge nationwide merchandise sales almost every year, a Final Four tournament appearance can take a relatively unknown school, such as Davidson or Austin Peay, and give them their fifteen minutes of fame. Remember George Mason, the school formerly best known for its originalist constitutional law program and 1500 SAT scores? The suburban Washington, D.C., commuter school was the Cinderella story of the 2006 Final Four, selling thirty thousand T-shirts in the month leading up to the tournament. Its merchandise sales were 800 percent ahead of LSU, the number one seed. There was a two-hour wait at the George Mason campus bookstore for merchandise. When a truck pulled up with more merchandise, students applauded.

"People are beside themselves," Carri Vitello, the textbook manager at the GMU Bookstore, told the Associated Press. "This is so new for us."

Indeed, Collegiate Licensing Corp. had a hard time getting retailers interested in George Mason apparel before the school's Final Four appearance. Pre-Final Four, only about ninety companies were licensed to make athletic apparel for the Fairfax, Virginia, school better known for its law school than its layups. GMU's distinguished alumni are in the Federalist Society, not the NFL. But the number of companies making—and selling—GMU merchandise more than quadrupled in the weeks following the school's 2006 Final Four appearance.

"A lot of our customers have asked to try and run a line of their products for George Mason all year-round," Bruce Johnson, manager of a Wal-Mart near the George Mason campus, told the Associated Press. In the wake of its tourney appearance, the school opened an online store at Gomason.com in affiliation with College Sports TV, selling everything from hats to golf balls.

And don't dare sport a logo during March Madness that isn't official. During the 2007 regional finals, North Carolina coach Roy Williams came into a press conference with a drink cup that had the wrong logo on it. The NCAA made him get rid of it right then and there.

"We have kids getting killed in a foreign country, and (they're) worried about me pouring a drink in an NCAA-sponsored cup," Williams said during a subsequent press conference.

IT'S ALL ABOUT SHOES

In short, like much of college sports today, March Madness is about money. And while most of that money comes from the folks at home and on the Internet who are mesmerized every March, wondering if Gonzaga will make it to the Elite 8 or Kentucky will even make it to the Sweet 16, the real business of March Madness is taking place a few blocks away at the National Association of Basketball Coaches Forum. This is where many of the side deals between the coaches, the schools, and the shoe companies are negotiated. It's where the Rick Pitinos and Coach K's of the world show up between games and practices to pose for photos with Nike execs and sign multimillion-dollar shoe and apparel contracts with Adidas. It's also where the coaches of tomorrow, the ones who are still coaching in high school or Division III, come to work out deals for their own programs and dream that one day it will be them standing up there, signing a $10 million multiyear deal.

If there's one man who's responsible for all this, it's Sonny Vaccaro. The short, round, balding Italian kid from a steel mill town in western Pennsylvania single-handedly created the multibillion-dollar branded apparel business that drives March Madness. In 1965, he created the Dapper Dan Roundball Classic in Pittsburgh. The tournament quickly became the premier showcase for up-and-coming high school players who hoped that demonstrating their skills before Vaccaro and the slew of scouts, coaches, and reporters who flocked to his tournament every year would get them a coveted NCAA D-I scholarship.

In 1977, Vaccaro approached a young entrepreneur named Phil Knight, who'd started a little shoe company in Portland, Oregon, called Nike. Basically, Vaccaro told Knight that if he could get the elite high school, college, and pro players to start wearing Nikes at his camps and on playgrounds across the country, they could dethrone Converse, which at the time was the reigning champion of basketball shoes and apparel. And Vaccaro knew exactly how to do it. Start paying college coaches to make their players wear Nike shoes. And it worked.

Knight and Vaccaro later expanded the business model that was targeted at what's supposed to be amateur athletics by paying the schools as well as the coaches. In exchange for a little payola and some swag, the schools would put the Nike Swoosh on their players' uniforms, just one more brand image for everyone at the stadium and—more important—watching on television. The formula was so successful that even once-incorruptible Penn State, with its staid blue and white uniforms and no names on the backs of jerseys, began sporting the Nike Swoosh.

In 1992, Vaccaro left Nike and went to Adidas and did the same thing all over again. He then moved on to Reebok, where he retired in January 2007 at age sixty-seven as the director of grassroots basketball. Why'd he quit? He was ashamed of himself. He was ashamed of the business he'd created. He was ashamed of how he and the schools and the sneaker companies had made money off of these kids all these years. In short, he was ashamed of what he'd done to basketball. He'd taken it from an innocent pickup game on countless street corners and schoolyards across America and turned it into a multibillion-dollar business, mostly built off the backs of the free labor of high school and college athletes, many of whom were poor black kids from the inner city. Whether you think Sonny Vaccaro is a modern-day Paul of Tarsus who suddenly had his epiphany or simply an unrepentant huckster who is finally coming to grips with his own mortality and is regretting a life of dirty deeds and ill-gotten gains, his story is compelling. In 2007, as part of his self-imposed penance, he began touring business schools around the country and telling everyone how he'd done it.

"When I started at Nike in 1977, there were no rules," he told an April 2007 audience at Duke Law School. "They had $25 million in sales and gave shoes to runners."

In fact, Vaccaro said, the few kids who wore them at his summer basketball camp pronounced it "Nicky." That's because in 1977 Converse "owned everything in marketing in basketball. Why? Because no one challenged them."

At the time, Converse wasn't paying coaches but was sponsoring their summer basketball camps. They would come in and provide shoes for the elite summer basketball camps that were named for coaches at places such as Kentucky and North Carolina. It was the primary source of outside income for college basketball coaches and didn't require much time. It was also totally legal in the eyes of the NCAA.

Big-name college basketball coaches would simply put their name on the camp and show up for a half-hour pep talk at the start and finish, and in between, the drills and scrimmages were run by graduate assistants. Converse paid the coaches a small fee for the right to come in and talk to the kids about their products, give them some freebies, and hopefully leave them with a favorable impression of the brand. This was the business model that Sonny Vaccaro wanted Nike to challenge in 1977.

So he flew to Oregon on his own dime and left a half dozen pairs of basketball shoes he'd designed with Knight. They looked more like sandals than basketball sneakers, and were totally impractical and unmarketable. But Knight was impressed with Vaccaro's drive and ambition. So he gave him some of Nike's basketball shoes, which Vaccaro proceeded to hand out to players on the street courts in New York, Chicago, and Los Angeles, where scouts would often discover unknown talent in those days. He went to streetball meccas like the courts at West Fourth Street and Sixth Avenue in Greenwich Village, where some of the best pickup ball is played by some of the best players in the country. And he went to pickup games in neighborhoods across the river, in Newark, where white guys were rarely seen. In fact, the few who wandered in—most of them lost—were lucky to get out alive. But Vaccaro was different. The fast-talking Italian street kid had what we call "street cred."

"Highly recruited players develop a keen sense real early about who is trying to help them and who is trying to get in their pocket," Antoine Walker, whom Vaccaro eventually lured to Adidas, told *Sports Illustrated.* "And Sonny has always come off as only wanting to help."

"I was nobody coming out of high school," Shaquille O'Neal told *ESPN the Magazine.* "But he always treated me nice. The better-known players got everything—jackets and bags. But I was in a mismatched pair of raggedy shoes, and he made a phone call to get me a pair of size 17s."

This is the guy who came knocking on Nike's door in 1977.

"They took me to a Chinese restaurant for lunch," he said. "Kept my shoes. Then I didn't hear from them for months."

Eventually, Nike called back.

"How do we get involved in basketball?" Vaccaro remembers them asking.

"Pay these guys," he told them, referring to the coaches.

"We can't pay these guys."

"There's no rule against it."

That would be Sonny Vaccaro's business model for the next three decades. Pushing the envelope. Always looking for the angle. And, he argues, always looking out for the kids, who, he quickly learned, were being exploited by a system that was more about television ratings and advertising revenue than reading, writing, and arithmetic.

After getting the go ahead from Nike, the first college basketball coach Vaccaro signed was his old friend Jerry Tarkanian at UNLV. According to Vaccaro, the whole contract was negotiated in five sentences.

"You're going to give me $5,000?" Tarkanian asked.

"Yes."

"You're going to give me shoes?"

"Yes."

"Where do I sign?"

When he offered a sneaker deal to Jim Valvano at Iona, it only took four sentences.

"You're going to give me a check?"

"Yes."

"Can I cash it?"

"Yes."

(Interestingly, Valvano was forced out of North Carolina State in 1989, six years after his Wolfpack squad was the Cinderella story at March Madness and went on to win the national championship. What most people didn't know was that most of his players were selling their free sneakers and basketball tickets and pocketing the money, a violation of NCAA rules.)

When Vaccaro started signing college coaches to shoe contracts, he had no budget from Nike. He'd sign a coach, write a check, and then wire Nike for the money. Because it took a week for the checks he was writing to clear, Vaccaro just managed to stay in the black.

"That's how it started," Vaccaro said. "I would sign the guy. I would call Phil. They would transfer the money."

Then *Washington Post* reporter Mark Asher wrote a story with the headline "Nike Paying College Coaches."

Nike panicked.

"The *Washington Post* says we're paying coaches," a Nike exec said to Vaccaro over the phone.

"We *are* paying coaches."

While Nike was worried about its image, Vaccaro was elated.

"This is the greatest thing that ever happened to us," he told Nike. "The *Washington Post* wrote about us."

In fact, the paper mentioned Vaccaro's deal with Valvano, but mistakenly said he coached at Iowa, not little-known Iona.

"The Iowa coach called Valvano and asked, 'How can I get one of these deals?'" Vaccaro recalls with a chuckle.

The story pretty much ended there; Nike endured a week of questions, then proceeded to sign shoe and apparel contracts with 910 schools.

"You've got it made," Vaccaro told Nike. "You own basketball."

In 1983, Vaccaro came up with the idea of signing a whole school, not just the high-profile football or basketball teams. The strategy was brilliant. It solved the one problem that frustrated every athletic director in the country. In short, they had to siphon off money from their revenue-generating sports like football and basketball to support the rest of the athletic department. This included sports that generated no revenue and drew audiences in the hundreds, not hundreds of thousands—soccer, rowing, wrestling, and the slew of Title IX-mandated women's sports.

"I got a million dollars and spread it around to my coaches," Vaccaro said. "If I gave a coach $20,000, I didn't care who got it. Soccer, football, baseball. We got a whole school for the price we would have paid a basketball coach."

AIR JORDAN IS BORN

A year later, Nike wanted to expand its sports merchandising and shoe contracts. It was looking at the Olympics and the NBA. At the time, professional basketball was nowhere near what it is today.

"It was the most meaningless professional sport in mankind," Vaccaro said of the NBA. "Most of the guys were doing drugs. The title games were on tape delay on the West Coast."

Nike wanted to give the money to the top players selected in the NBA Draft. That year, they were Charles Barkley, Sam Bowie, and a still relatively unknown kid from North Carolina named Michael Jordan.

"Give it all to Jordan," Vaccaro told Nike.

"I'd never met him," Vaccaro said. "He didn't come to my camps. But I said, 'Give it all to the kid.'"

"Would you bet your job on it?" Nike asked.

"Yes. Sign the kid."

So Vaccaro set up a meeting at the L'Ermitage Hotel in Beverly Hills with Jordan and his agent, David Falk. He offered Jordan a $250,000 signing bonus and 25 cents for every Air Jordan shoe that Nike sold. Falk came back with $500,000 and five cents a shoe. This, Vaccaro said, was when he first realized he was in a less-than-altruistic business.

"David Falk got 10 percent of the $500,000, but nothing from the shoe royalties," he said. "The best deal for Michael was 25 cents a shoe, but the agent was thinking of himself, not his client. That woke me up."

It didn't take long for Jordan to wake up, either. On his second shoe contract he demanded that Nike make him a partner in the Air Jordan brand. That's what really kicked the whole endorsement business into high gear. Before, it was the schools and coaches that were getting the money, mainly because NCAA rules don't allow players to be paid. But it was Jordan's personal endorsement deal with Nike—albeit after his college career—that told kids on every court in the country that they, too, could become basketball millionaires with their own shoe brand. And while the odds of that happening were slim to none, Nike didn't care. Neither did the colleges or the coaches. Even the kids who knew the odds thought they could beat them.

"I'll be the one," they thought. That image, that idea, sold shoes. And Nike made a killing.

"The whole endorsement world started with Jordan," Vaccaro said. "It's why LeBron [James] got a $100 million deal. Because of Michael Jordan. And the craziest thing is that if David Falk wouldn't have done what he'd done, the Jordan brand would have taken off sooner and Nike would have been poorer."

Vaccaro went on to be one of the most powerful brokers in all of college athletics. Thanks to the business model he created, LeBron James, an eighteen-year-old high school kid from Akron, Ohio, who opted to go straight from high school to the NBA, signed a five-year, $90 million contract with Nike in 2003. To put that in context, the deal was just shy of the five-year, $100 million contract Nike had with Tiger Woods. And LeBron James hadn't even stepped onto an NBA court yet.

To put LeBron's deal in historical context, Jordan's first contract with Nike was eventually valued at about $2.5 million. Shaquille O'Neal's deal with Reebok in 1992 was for $3 million. Kobe Bryant's deal with Adidas in 1996 was for $5 million. And Sonny Vaccaro had a hand in them all.

So how big is the athletic shoe and apparel business today? In a 2007 SEC filing, Nike revealed that it had $2.5 billion in endorsement obligations going forward. It expected to pay $462 million in 2008, $418 million in 2009, $337 million in 2010, $276 million in 2011, and $887 million in the out years.

With the shoe companies behind him, Vaccaro turned his summer basketball camps into showcases for the best high school talent in the country. The scouts and media came to write about the kids, the shoe companies salivated over their next crop of prospects, and the kids left with duffle bags full of Nike-, Adidas-, and Reebok-branded shorts, t-shirts, warmups, caps, and, of course, sneakers. This is the financial model that has fueled March Madness and made it the second-biggest sporting event in the country.

AGAIN, THE COACHES CASH IN

In Chapter 7, we'll look at coaches' salaries, and you'll see that, by far, the largest share of their multimillion-dollar compensation packages come from side deals, not salary. These include hosting basketball camps, speaking to booster clubs, and sneaker and apparel contracts. Marquette basketball coach Tom Crean's compensation included money from Nike for the school's apparel and shoe contract. While Crean's take from Nike was small potatoes—"Not at the level you read about," Marquette spokesman Mike Broeker said during a press conference—some of the endorsement deals are worth millions of dollars.

Duke's Coach K has a fifteen-year, $6 million sponsorship contract with Nike. When Rick Pitino left the University of Kentucky to coach the NBA's Boston Celtics, he earned $3.3 million a year in salary, endorsements, radio and TV deals, and summer camps. When he returned to coach the Louisville Cardinals, his total compensation package was valued at more than $12 million, with most of it coming from side deals. Arizona's title-winning coach, Lute Olson, earns $300,000 from a shoe contract.

Some universities have prohibited direct contracts between coaches and apparel companies. Instead, the money from Nike, Reebok, Adidas, and others is paid directly to the university. The Big Ten Conference has a policy that bans contracts between shoe companies and coaches. The Big East lets individual schools decide what is best.

The bottom line is this: beyond the headlines and dollar figures, shoe and apparel contracts can mean big money for colleges and universities (see Table 4.1).

Florida State became the eighth school to reach an agreement on an all-university contract with Nike. Miami University was the first to sign such a deal with the nation's leading producer of athletic footwear, which has

TABLE 4.1

Some Recent All-School Endorsement Deals with Nike

School	Endorsement	Years
FSU	$6 million	5 years
Michigan	$5.7 million	6 years
North Carolina	$4.69 million	4 years
Alabama	$2.9 million	5 years
Penn State	$2.6 million	4 years
Illinois	$2.5 million	7 years

Source: Author's research.

recently put added emphasis on its apparel and sideline wear marketing. It's clear what Nike gets out of the deal. Players from these big-name programs are seen wearing the Nike Swoosh, which in turn drives sales at retail outlets. But how does the university use the money? Again, the answers are not what you'd think.

In addition to the $6 million Nike pays Florida State, it makes a $100,000 contribution to the University Capital Campaign through the purchase of a skybox at Doak Campbell Stadium. Nike also gave $750,000 to the university to be used exclusively for minority and women's programs, as well as a degree-completion program for former athletes.

"It gives the university and president the discretion to take those dollars, as it relates to some of the scholarship areas that we've designated, that we'll be able to match some of those monies," FSU athletic director Dave Hart said.

Under the terms of the contract, Nike also pays $225,000 annually as part of football coach Bobby Bowden's contract. The agreement with Nike was one of the factors that delayed completion of Bowden's new five-year contract, which pays him $1 million a year.

Basketball coach Pat Kennedy receives $150,000 and baseball coach Mike Martin $15,000 from Nike as part of the financial package. Under the agreement, FSU retains its ownership of registered trademarks such as the Seminole Indian logo, and merchants still will be allowed to sell FSU sportswear with the Seminole logo on it. In 2006, FSU was number two in merchandise sold nationally, behind the University of Michigan.

"I am really pleased with the agreement and the partnership as it relates to the entire program," Hart said. "I think the contract is a good one in the sense that it not only benefits athletics but also the university."

Here are some of the other terms of the FSU agreement.

The cheerleaders, dance team, and even athletic administrators will be supplied with Nike attire. In return, FSU will provide to Nike

Up to thirty tickets to each of two home football games designated by the university

Up to twelve tickets to bowl games in which the football team is a participant

Up to six season tickets to men's and women's home basketball games
Up to twenty-five tickets to one home men's and women's basketball
   game designated by the university

Nike gets signage at Doak Campbell Stadium and the Tallahassee-Leon County Civic Center, as well as logo recognition in media guides, sports-related publications, and videos generated by the university.

In 2008, Nike came out on top for the ninth consecutive year when it came to outfitting the postseason bowl teams. Nine of the ten squads competing in the five Bowl Championship Series games, and nearly 74 percent of the teams participating in bowl games in 2008, were wearing Nike apparel and shoes on the field.

A BUMP IN THE ROAD

Of course, sometimes sneaker deals don't always work out for the best. In 2005, Arkansas State's leading scorer sat out because he refused to wear Adidas shoes, which players are obligated to wear because of a school contract. Jerry Nichols, a six-foot, six-inch outside shooter who averaged 9.6 points per game, has had two knee operations. He said he was wearing Adidas shoes the first time he hurt the knee.

"I tore my ACL in Adidas in junior college back in 2001, and I'm not comfortable wearing Adidas," Nichols told the Associated Press.

The school insisted that Nichols dress according to the contract.

"We have a contractual agreement with Adidas, and it's not any different than any number of other contracts with other schools," Arkansas State athletic director Dean Lee said in a press release. "There is not any stipulation or any research that shows any shoes are worse than any others. Adidas shoes are part of our uniform," Lee said.

Nichols threatened to file suit.

"If I have to miss this whole senior season for some shoes, why wouldn't I (sue)?" Nichols said. "I have done too much this summer, working out, staying up here all summer to waste a year. So if it has to come to a legal issue then I will."

It didn't. Adidas eventually gave Arkansas State a waiver for Nichols—and Nichols only—to wear shoes other than Adidas.

"ASU has been released from its legal obligation to use Adidas only as it pertains to Jerry Nichols, a men's basketball player," Adidas said. "All other personnel are still bound by the terms of the university's contract with Adidas."

But for the most part, shoe and apparel companies hold schools to the terms of their contract. That's because they know that seeing the Nike Swoosh or the Reebok logo on a college star has a huge impact on what the kids wear on the playground.

"Everybody wanted to wear the shoes that were on TV," said North Carolina's Marcus Ginyard.

North Carolina, Jordan's alma mater, is one of six programs chosen by Jordan to wear the Jumpman logo. And Ginyard's size-14 shoes are just a tiny part of that multimillion-dollar deal. For the players, it's about wearing the latest $150 basketball shoes. For the university, it's about bringing millions of dollars into the athletic department. For Nike, it's about selling billions of dollars in shoes and apparel.

"It's kind of like the same formula you have in the NBA," said Josiah Lake, Nike senior product line manager for Jordan footwear. "Kids will look up to these guys, especially at a North Carolina or a Georgetown. They automatically look to their feet to see what they have on."

Carolina is one of about a dozen schools with an all-sports apparel contract with Nike. Under the eight-year, $28.3 million deal signed in 2001, Nike supplies more than $2 million worth of shoes and Swoosh-embossed apparel and equipment per year for twenty-eight Tar Heels sports teams. That includes about $58,500 a year for the North Carolina men's basketball team. Carolina coach Roy Williams also has a $500,000 deal with Nike. Other cash from the contract goes to the athletics department's general fund and to the Chancellor's Academic Enhancement Fund.

Duke is also a Nike school, while North Carolina State's men's basketball program gets about $30,000 worth of shoes, apparel, and equipment from Adidas each year.

"It's just tremendous for us, not only from the value that we receive, but the quality of the shoes and the apparel that we receive," said Carolina athletic director Dick Baddour.

Nike had revenue of $18.6 billion in fiscal year 2008, up from $16.3 billion the year before and $13.7 billion in 2005. Included in those figures is an estimated $300 million from Air Jordan. While all of the shoe companies declined to talk about their shoe and sports apparel business, Nike spokesman Rodney Knox said that "the hope for us is that the visibility of the program translates to basketball fans, people that love to play."

And, of course, buy shoes.

5 MUD ROOMS AND ELECTRON MICROSCOPES

In the blistering summer heat of 2006, second-year head football coach Charlie Weis was putting the Notre Dame squad through its paces at Cartier Field, the team's practice facility in South Bend. After their grueling two-hour practice sessions in the humid Midwest heat, their entire bodies drenched in sweat, the players returned to the air-conditioned comfort of the palatial Guglielmino Athletics Complex. Affectionately referred to as "The Gug" (pronounced "The Goog"), the new building houses the football practice week locker rooms, coaches' offices, and meeting rooms, as well as expanded sports medicine, strength and conditioning, and weight room areas for all eight hundred Notre Dame student-athletes.

"The Gug" is one of the top training facilities in the country—college or professional. The 25,000-square-foot Haggar Fitness Center has over 250 pieces of weight training equipment, six plasma-screen televisions, a state-of-the-art sound system, a fifty-yard track for speed workouts, and an 810-square-yard Prestige Turf field for team stretching exercises and workouts. There's also an 8,260-square-foot athletic training center with two swim exercise pools, one of which has a treadmill on the bottom. Also on the main floor are locker rooms for the football players and coaching staff, as well as a player's lounge, nine team position group-meeting rooms, and a five hundred-seat auditorium with extra-large seating to accommodate Notre Dame's three-hundred-pound linemen. To keep the plush carpeting clean, there's an anterior "mud room," where players take off their cleats before coming inside. The 125 lockers feature special cleat warmers-driers.

The second-floor offices encompass about 7,700 square feet. Weis's suite, which includes two offices, a conference room, and a private bath and shower, overlooks Cartier Field. The offices for assistant coaches are off of two long hallways labeled "Defense" and "Offense." The video coordinator's compound sits in the center of it all and is linked into every room in the building.

There's also a recruiting lounge on the second floor that's decorated with eleven national championship banners and a balcony with a panoramic view of Notre Dame's central campus. It is this view—and these facilities—that undoubtedly got Jimmy Clausen, the most highly recruited quarterback to come out of Southern California since John Elway, and others to sign their letters of intent to the Catholic university run by the Brothers of the Holy Cross (not the Jesuits, as is commonly thought). Altogether, the $21.25 million practice facility built for what are supposed to be amateur athletes encompasses some 95,840 square feet.

At the same time that coach Weis was putting his team through blocking and tackling drills, across campus a team of carpenters, electricians, and computer programmers were putting the finishing touches on the Jordan Hall of Science. The $70 million, 200,000-square-foot state-of-the-art facility includes forty undergraduate laboratories for biology, chemistry, and physics; two 250-seat lecture halls; a 150-seat multimedia lecture hall; two classrooms; offices for faculty and pre-professional (pre-med) studies; a greenhouse; a herbarium; and an observatory.

"The Jordan Hall of Science," then–Notre Dame president Father Edward Malloy said during a press conference, "will provide our undergraduates with a superb learning environment, and it will free space in other buildings for our growing research efforts in the sciences."

The crown jewel of Jordan Hall is the Digital Visualization Theater. It has 136 seats and a 360-degree domed ceiling, similar to a planetarium.

"The reason we call it the Digital Visualization Theater rather than a planetarium is because it is intended to serve all the sciences and even Notre Dame students in fields outside of science," said Dennis C. Jacobs, the Notre Dame Chemistry professor who oversaw the project. "Students will be able to experience what it is like to be inside a cell, or see the transcription of DNA to messenger RNA, or to experience what it would be like to visit King Tut's tomb.

"A chemist might say, 'here's a target molecule we're trying to develop for cancer therapy,' then electronically transfer the graphics file to the master computer," Jacobs said. "A cluster of microprocessors then performs a real-time 3-D rendering of the target molecule and projects it on the dome. As the enormous molecule rotates or moves across the dome at the instructor's command, students feel as if they have been transported into the molecule's universe. They can begin to appreciate how subtle changes in the linkages between a few atoms can impact the molecule's three-dimensional structure and its subsequent reactivity. The astrophysics faculty are ecstatic that they now can have their students fly through space and visit any corner of the galaxy. These astronomical journeys can be scripted in advance or driven in real time at the whim of the instructor. The Digital Visualization Theater leaves students with an indelible image of the intricacies of nature."

Together, the Guglielmino Athletics Complex and the Jordan Hall of Science are two of the most impressive new buildings on the Notre Dame campus. But it may surprise many to learn that only one of them was paid for by funds including money generated by the football program.

"The Gug" was a gift from the family of Don F. Guglielmino. A long-time supporter of Notre Dame, he only attended the university for one year, 1939–40. When his father died he was forced to return to his native California and enrolled at Stanford. Then World War II came along. He left school to enlist in the Army Air Corps and served with distinction in the Pacific. After the war, Guglielmino returned to his hometown of Glendale, California, where he started Newhall Hardware in 1947. He helped found the Santa Clarita National Bank in the mid-1960s and was the bank's chairman until it was sold to Security Pacific National Bank in 1990 (and later acquired by Bank of America).

Before his death in 2001, Guglielmino had been a regular contributor to the Notre Dame Club of Los Angeles scholarship fund, the university's Institute for Church Life, and the football program. He was recognized as an honorary alumnus in 1996 and was inducted into Notre Dame's prestigious Monogram Club after his death.

"Though Don spent just a year at Notre Dame as a student, he had a great love for our university," Father Malloy said.

Jordan Hall was primarily underwritten by John W. Jordan II. A 1969 Notre Dame graduate and a member of the university's Board of Trustees, he is the founder of The Jordan Company, a private investment firm. He is also chairman and chief executive officer of Jordan Industries Inc., a Chicago-based holding company. Previous donations include the Jordan Auditorium, part of Notre Dame's Mendoza College of Business. As a member of the Board of Trustees, Jordan chairs the investment committee, which oversees the university's endowment.

Although the vast majority of the money needed to build Jordan Hall came from Mr. Jordan himself, the science center was partially funded by the $14.5 million that Notre Dame received from appearing in the 2006 Fiesta Bowl. Indeed, Notre Dame used all of its Fiesta Bowl money for purely academic—not athletic—purposes. More specifically, it was used for undergraduate and graduate financial aid, for library acquisitions, and to purchase scientific instruments for Jordan Hall.

TABLE 5.1

What Conferences Get from Television

Conference	Total revenue	Conference	Total revenue
Southeastern Conference	$122,488,264	Horizon League	$2,546,121
Big Ten Conference	$116,988,912	West Coast Conference	$2,376,684
Atlantic Coast Conference	$109,117,674	Metro Atlantic Athletic	
Big 12 Conference	$98,164,119	Conference	$2,373,926
Pacific-10 Conference	$73,148,851	Southern Conference	$2,139,320
Big East Conference	$68,465,385	Ohio Valley Conference	$1,938,448
Conference USA	$30,111,098	America East Conference	$1,929,010
Mid-American Conference	$8,047,309	Big Sky Conference	$1,889,678
Atlantic 10 Conference	$7,960,648	Big South Conference	$1,872,036
Western Athletic Conference	$5,615,518	Atlantic Sun Conference	$1,817,488
Missouri Valley Conference	$5,250,702	Colonial Athletic Association	$1,778,964
Mountain West Conference	$4,487,207	Southland Conference	$1,657,904
Sun Belt Conference[a]	$3,423,037	Patriot League	$1,566,255
Southwestern Athletic		Big West Conference[a]	$1,305,431
Conference	$2,839,158	Northeast Conference[a]	$1,208,201

Source: Conference filings with the Internal Revenue Service. Revenues reported by athletics conferences in Division I of the National Collegiate Athletic Association for the 2002–3 fiscal year, except as noted. The Mid-Continent Conference and the Mid-Eastern Athletic Conference did not respond to repeated requests for data. The Ivy League is not incorporated as a not-for-profit organization and is not required to file Internal Revenue Service Form 990s.

[a]Data from 2001–2 fiscal year.

"We're, of course, pleased that our team has competed at such a high level this year and is being rewarded with this bowl opportunity," said Father John Jenkins, who was named Notre Dame's president in 2005. "But we're also very grateful that the funds from our participation will go to address such important needs for the academic mission of the university."

Unfortunately, Notre Dame is the exception, not the rule. Only a handful of college athletic departments turn a profit. The rest either break even or rely on student activity fees, alumni donations, and other money to operate.

That doesn't mean that television revenue isn't important to understanding the economics of college athletics. It is. In this chapter, you'll learn that television is by far the greatest source of revenue for the two collegiate sports that generate the most money: basketball and football. The NCAA's $6.1 billion television contract with CBS to broadcast March Madness represents almost 90 percent of the total money the NCAA earns from college basketball. And, as Table 5.1 shows, television provides a lucrative source of revenues for the various athletic conferences each year.

BROADCAST BOUNTY

Television broadcast revenues aren't sufficient enough to generate huge profits for most college athletic departments, but they are often the difference between just breaking even and being deep in the red. For many schools, revenues from broadcast rights often mean that athletic directors don't have to go to their college presidents and ask that money be diverted to athletics from the general academic and operating funds.

Television also is primarily responsible for providing the money needed to support non-revenue sports, especially Title IX–mandated women's programs. This is especially true when it comes to March Madness. Although women's basketball has its own sixty-four-team tournament, only two of the elite women's teams consistently earn a profit: Connecticut and Tennessee. The rest of the women's Division I teams that appear in the annual tournament are supported by the television revenues that are generated by football and men's basketball.

Of course, all this television money comes at a price. In addition to participants being slaves to the network schedulers, many critics see television as the single biggest driving force today behind the gross commercialization of big-time college athletics. They have a point. Without television, there wouldn't be an audience of tens of millions of fans to see the Nike Swoosh that's prominently displayed on players' uniforms. Without this explosion of naming rights and sponsorships, we'd all be sitting down on January 1 to watch games that used to be simply known as "The Cotton Bowl," (now the "AT&T Cotton Bowl") the Sugar Bowl (now the "Allstate Sugar Bowl"), and the Peach Bowl (now the "Chick-fil-A Bowl"). And, of course, without television, universities wouldn't be compelled to produce self-serving, hypocritical public service announcements that falsely proclaim that their student-athletes really do care more about biochemistry than basketball.

"Driven by the insatiable public demand for entertainment, the commercial nature of the news, broadcasting, and the entertainment industry, and the feverish hype of the sports press, our two most prominent college sports, football and basketball, have been transformed into big-time show business," wrote former University of Michigan president James J. Duderstadt in his excellent book, *Intercollegiate Athletics and the American University.*

"Players and coaches have become celebrities," he wrote. "Athletic events have become media products. The objectives of these college sports activities have become market share and commercial value, and the welfare of their players as students has been largely ignored. Any educational mission—indeed, relevance of these programs to the rest of the university—has been subverted if not destroyed entirely."

In many ways, Duderstadt is right. And while it's true that the modern national broadcast television contract began in 1991 with Notre Dame and NBC—and has ballooned out of all proportion since—it's also true that broadcast rights were an important part of the economics of college sports long before Joe Paterno started stomping up and down the sidelines in his signature white socks and black cleats, or ABC's Keith Jackson started yelling "Whoa, Nellie," from the broadcast booth at Michigan Stadium, which he dubbed, "The Big House."

FIRST THERE WAS RADIO

Decades before television, of course, there was radio. The first college football game broadcast was on the student-run radio station at the University of Minnesota in 1912. Eight years later, the first commercial college sports broadcast was on WTAW in College Station, Texas. In 1922, the Princeton-Chicago football game was the first "nationally broadcast" game, carried over a telephone wire that ran from New York to Chicago. In 1926, NBC inked the first network radio deal for college sports. A year later, it broadcast the Rose Bowl for the first time.

It didn't take long for colleges and universities across the country to discover the value in a radio broadcast contract. Radio not only brought in revenue but also built a following for the school well beyond its ivy-covered walls. Radio broadcasts helped alumni keep tabs on their alma mater, no matter where they lived. It also built huge followings among fans who had never attended those schools. This is especially true in states that have one predominant state university, such as Indiana, Iowa, and Minnesota. Long before Minnesota was "The State of Hockey," the University of Minnesota's games were broadcast across the state, making nearly everyone a Gopher fan.

Duderstadt's University of Michigan initially took the high road when it came to radio broadcast rights. In the 1920s and 1930s, Michigan games were broadcast for free. But by 1935, Michigan had recognized the obvious commercial advantages and was earning $20,000 a year from radio broadcast rights. When the Big Ten Conference tried to negotiate a conference-wide broadcast agreement, Michigan was one of its staunchest opponents. Why? It would have meant getting $10,000 a year from a $100,000 contract split ten ways instead of the $20,000 Michigan was getting on its own.

Yale had a $20,000 broadcast contract at the time as well. This drew the ire of both Harvard and Princeton, who each had turned down offers of $65,000 for two years. Left out in the cold, the two Ivy League schools suddenly rediscovered their ethics—if they had ever had any—and accused Yale of buying into the "commercial atmosphere which already surrounds intercollegiate athletics to a troublesome degree."

The only school that consistently adhered to the free broadcast model was Notre Dame. As noted sports economist Andrew Zimbalist wrote in his excellent book, *Unpaid Professionals:* "Notre Dame believed that not only was this the proper policy for amateur sports and that it was congruent with the school's religious commitment, but serendipitously the policy would also allow more fans to follow Notre Dame games, yielding positive publicity for the university."

Indeed, in many ways, it was the free broadcast rights—and the team's phenomenal success on the field—that made Notre Dame the closest thing we've ever had to a national college football team (I say "had" because of Notre Dame's abysmal record since Lou Holtz left, including the past few seasons under vaunted coach Charlie Weis).

When television came along, athletic directors and college presidents immediately saw the value in broadcasting rights. The first televised college game was a 1939 baseball game between Princeton and Columbia. A year later, Penn began broadcasting its football games locally.

Many college presidents and athletic directors worried that broadcasting games on television would hurt the gate. So many of the early college contracts had clauses that paid damages to the schools for lost tickets revenue.

As television grew through the late 1940s and 1950s, so too did the number of collegiate television contracts. Wisconsin got $10,000 a year, Tulane $7,500, USC and UCLA $34,500 each. Oklahoma sold its television rights for just $10, but also got a percentage of the profits. Even Notre Dame started cashing in. In 1948, the Catholic university sold the broadcast rights to its game against Navy for $21,000. A year later, the price rose to $36,000 plus incentives.

This all worked quite well until 1951. That's when Penn signed a three-year, $850,000 television broadcast contract with the fledgling Du Mont television network. At the NCAA Convention that year, delegates, incensed over the size of the Penn contract (and probably a little bit jealous), voted 161 to 7 to restrict what had been known as "home rule," which allowed schools to negotiate their own radio and television rights. Penn president Harold Stassen protested the ruling, saying it violated the Sherman Antitrust Act. The NCAA in turn ruled that Penn was no longer in good standing, and many of the Ivy League schools agreed, saying they would not play Penn. Pressured from all sides, Penn relented and cancelled the contract with Du Mont.

Although the majority of NCAA delegate schools were able to defeat Penn over its lucrative television deal, they lost home rule. The big winner to emerge out of the whole affair was the NCAA. Now it would not only negotiate national television rights but also set the schedule.

The first NCAA-negotiated deal was with Westinghouse in 1951 for $679,000. A year later, the NCAA signed a $1.1 million contract with NBC. And that's the way college football television rights were negotiated for the next four decades.

It wasn't a bad plan. From 1951 to 1983, annual broadcast revenue rose from $1.1 million to $74.1 million. The NCAA kept about 10 percent for expenses, and the rest was distributed to teams in a proportional revenue-sharing model. In short, the more times you were on television, the bigger your cut of the pie.

This worked great for schools such as Michigan, Notre Dame, and Alabama, but it hurt the smaller schools. And the television networks' East Coast myopia hurt the Pac-10 and other conferences out west. No network was going to delay lucrative and popular Saturday night programming at 7:00 P.M. Eastern time to show the Washington-Cal game that started at 4:00 P.M. on the West Coast.

TELEVISION RIGHTS REVOLT

In 1973, the NCAA tried to more equitably distribute television revenues by separating the elite Division I schools from the smaller D-II and D-III programs. Under the deal, the NCAA would give the smaller schools $500,000 of the $16 million national television pact. As one-sided as the deal seems, it would have marked a significant increase in broadcast revenue for the smaller schools. But they balked, saying that it didn't fix the fundamental problem: the rich were getting richer and the poor were getting nothing.

Two years later, Cal State-Long Beach president Stephen Horn made a radical proposal at the NCAA's Annual Meeting. He wanted the NCAA to give half of the television contract money to schools that never appeared on television. His argument was that the money would allow them to build up their football programs, be competitive, and appear more on television. When they rose to the top, other lesser teams would get the bigger payout that they'd been receiving.

The proposal was given a solid thumbs down by the cabal of college presidents who represented the biggest football programs in the country and thus controlled the NCAA committee that oversaw television rights. But the proposal started a serious discussion about the collectivist nature of the consolidation of college football broadcasting rights. It also set the stage for a momentous sea change, the effects of which are still being felt today.

Chafing under the yoke of the NCAA's central control, the major conferences—the Big Ten, the Pac-10, and the SEC—realized that they were the real power brokers when it came to television broadcast rights. They controlled the talent, the venues, and the fans. Without them, the NCAA national broadcast contract was worthless. So in 1981 they set up their own organization, the Collegiate Football Association, and negotiated their own deal with ABC. Three years later, the Supreme Court ruled that the NCAA's central control over college sports broadcasting rights amounted to restraint of trade. The days of centralized broadcast rights and scheduling were over.

"The floodgates opened," writes Michigan's Duderstadt. "Several conferences, including the Big Ten and Pac-10, were powerful enough to negotiate their own television contracts. The CFA continued for a few more years, but it eventually disintegrated when Notre Dame negotiated its own contract with NBC and withdrew from the CFA."

Indeed, Notre Dame was the first to sign an individual national broadcast contract, with NBC Sports in 1991. It was, in many ways, the beginning of the modern era of college sports broadcasting.

In 2004, Notre Dame and NBC signed their fourth contract extension, a five-year deal that will pay Notre Dame $9 million for broadcast rights to all of the home games from South Bend from 2006 through 2010. And because Notre Dame is one of the most storied—and well-supported—college football programs in the country, much of the NBC money, like the 2006 Fiesta Bowl money, has gone to support academics. As a result, scholarships funded by Notre Dame's television revenue increased tenfold from 1991 to 2004, from $5.4 million to $53.7 million.

"While our partnership with NBC has been important to Irish athletics, it is the general student body that has been the greatest beneficiary," Father Malloy said in an interview. "From the very beginning, the majority of revenue generated through the contract with NBC has been directed toward the financial aid needs of our students. Now, thanks to this innovative collaboration, the dream of a Notre Dame education has been made a reality for hundreds of Notre Dame students who have received millions of dollars in scholarship support."

In the 2006–7 school year, there were 247 Notre Dame undergraduates receiving need-based scholarships, averaging $13,000 each, funded by revenue from the NBC television contract. Since its inception, the contract has funded 1,920 Notre Dame undergraduate students to the tune of $20 million in need-based and academic financial aid. Notre Dame has used $5.5 million to endow doctoral fellowships in its graduate school. Earnings from the endowment are used for graduate teaching fellows, a minority fellowship program, and summer research fellowships. Nearly $4 million from the NBC contract has been used to endow MBA scholarships at the Mendoza College of Business. Since 1994, nearly 200 MBA students have been supported through the NBC endowment. During the 2005–6 academic year, fourteen students were designated as NBC fellows.

Unfortunately, there has been a downside to the Notre Dame-NBC contract. Everyone wants one. And in many ways they've gotten it. As Table 5.1 shows, every major (and minor) athletic conference, from the SEC and Pac-10 to the Patriot League and the Big Sky, gets a substantial amount of money from television broadcast rights. Thus television has become the drug that fuels the addiction of college sports. And like an addict, many colleges don't care what they have to do to get it.

Furthermore, not every athletic director is as generous with his television money as the good brothers in South Bend. In short, most schools don't use television and sponsorship money generated by athletics to build libraries and fund scholarships. That's because there's a misperception among fans that most big-time college sports programs are awash in money, much of it coming from lucrative television contracts. It's true that the television contracts are often measured in the hundreds of millions of dollars, but the athletic departments spend the TV money as quickly as they can cash the check. They spend it on lavish locker rooms, recruiting trips on private jets, and the general expenses that come with running a big-time D-I program. As a result, many schools rely on their television money—whether it's self-generated or part of a conference-wide revenue-sharing plan—just to break even.

Many schools also use their television revenues from football and basketball to support other non-revenue sports, such as soccer, volleyball, and lacrosse. And with very few exceptions, those non-revenue sports include every women's team that's mandated by Title IX, the federal statute that says schools that receive federal funding must spend equal amounts of money on men's and women's athletics.

A good example is Louisiana State University. The LSU football team made about $11.3 million dollars in 2005. In fact, the program has made more than $11 million each year since 1999. Its banner year was 2003, when it made $19.1 million and won the national championship.

"Football is the engine that drives the train," LSU associate athletic director Mark Ewing told the Associated Press. "And the other sports know that."

Notice that I said the money that the "LSU football team" brought in, not profit. The athletic department breaks even. That's because the television money and other revenue that's generated by LSU football goes to support the other non-revenue sports.

Case in point is the LSU men's and women's basketball programs. If you do a thorough accounting of the LSU basketball program, and exclude television revenues, both the men's and women's basketball teams consistently lose money. According to the school, in 2005 the men's basketball team, which is nowhere near as successful as the football team, lost more than $100,000. What put it in the black was the $9.7 million the school received from television revenue sharing with the NCAA, the vast majority of which was generated by the LSU football team.

"Out of that $9 million, only $2.73 million is from men's basketball," Ewing said.

The same is true for the LSU women's basketball program, which is mandated by Title IX because the school fields a men's basketball team. In 2005, the LSU women's basketball team was in the red by about $1.3 million. The team has lost more than $1 million each year since 2001. Not even the arrival of all-star guard Seimone Augustus could put the program in the black. Her arrival resulted in a tenfold increase in ticket sales, but it was nowhere near enough to offset the total cost of the program.

In 2002, the LSU women's basketball team had ticket sales of $28,600. When Augustus joined the team a year later, ticket sales increased to $212,303 and by 2005 had climbed to $352,068. The team also makes about $50,000 a year in television revenue, for its own appearances as well as revenue it gets for playing in nationally televised games against Connecticut and Tennessee, the only two women's basketball programs in the country that consistently turn a profit. (In 2005, the University of Connecticut earned the most of any women's basketball program with a profit of about $1.6 million.)

Is the money that the LSU football team brings in part of the gross commercialization of college athletics? Absolutely. Would LSU still have a men's or women's basketball team without it. Probably. But LSU would have to get the money from somewhere. It would get it by either cutting other sports, increasing student fees, or asking wealthy alumni to help fund the programs.

The point is this: though a college president may be vehemently against the commercialization of college sports, he quickly realizes that he can't live without it. That's the Hobson's choice that's faced by college presidents and chancellors on campuses across this country every day.

TWO NEW TRENDS

Although the economic benefits of television broadcast rights are pretty clear, two issues roiled college sports broadcasting in 2007–8. One is the creation of the Big Ten Network, which could ultimately turn out to be the single biggest misstep by college sports in decades. The other is high school football on television.

The Big Ten Network

The Big Ten Network is a natural extension of the broadcast rights revolt that rocked college sports in the late 1970s and early 1980s. In short, the big D-I football conferences realized that they no longer needed the NCAA to negotiate television rights. In fact, they'd make more money if they didn't have to share revenue—albeit disproportionately—with the Slippery Rocks and Appalachian States of the world. While this model of schools and conferences negotiating for themselves has worked well for the big D-I conferences, the Big Ten Network may be the first example of a conference overplaying its hand.

The Big Ten Conference, the nonprofit group that negotiates broadcast deals for its eleven universities, formed the network with Fox in 2006. The conference owns 51 percent of the network; Fox owns the rest. The network bought the rights to four hundred Big Ten games for $50 million to $60 million a year. But it gets to show only the games that are not picked up by ESPN and ABC. The Disney networks have a separate ten-year, $1 billion deal to broadcast the most attractive Big Ten football and basketball games.

In addition to football, the Big Ten Network planned to broadcast at least 105 regular-season men's basketball games, 55 regular-season women's games, 170 other events from sports such as softball and track, and Big Ten championships during 2007–8. The network also owns the rights to tapes of Big Ten football and basketball games back to 1960, which allows it to produce shows similar to those featured on ESPN Classic.

The biggest problem for the Big Ten Network in its first year was accessiblity. And there wasn't a better example of that than the November 13, 2007, Wisconsin-Ohio State game. In years past, a game between the number-twenty-one-ranked Badgers and the number one Buckeyes would have been seen nationwide on ABC, ESPN, or ESPN2. But as Wisconsin and Ohio State lined up for the kickoff, the Big Ten Network had yet to strike a deal with Comcast, Time Warner, and other cable companies. As a result, most fans in Wisconsin and Ohio were unable to see the game in their own homes. That's because only 35 percent of the households in Wisconsin and

40 percent in Ohio were on cable or satellite systems that offered the Big Ten Network. In short, it was good for the neighborhood sports bar, but it was a disaster for the Big Ten Network and the vast majority of the Big Ten diaspora nationwide who couldn't sit at home and watch the game, which is the whole point of a nationwide network.

There were other mathematical formulae working against the Big Ten Network in its inaugural broadcast year. Although it had a respectable thirty million cable and satellite subscribers nationwide, Comcast, Time Warner, Charter, and Mediacom controlled 65 percent of the TV homes in the eight Big Ten states. None of those cable providers was in a hurry to meet the Big Ten Network's terms. That's because the Big Ten Network wanted the cable companies to pay $1.10 a month per subscriber and offer the network as part of its basic service. Comcast and others wanted to offer the Big Ten Network as part of a sports tier package that cost about $5 a month.

From a purely economic standpoint, this is interesting because it's basically a battle of wills between two entrenched monopolies. The Big Ten has a monopoly on the broadcast rights and the cable companies have a monopoly on the delivery system (and, apparently, never the two shall meet).

The Big Ten Network also wanted Comcast and other cable providers to pay rights fees based on the total number of subscribers in the eight Big Ten states. In short, it wanted every Comcast customer to pay for a network that only a fraction will watch.

Also, while the Big Ten has some of the most successful sports teams in the country, can you really fill twenty-four hours of programming with them? The Big Ten thought so. Instead of infomercials, the 2:00 A.M. hour features Iowa versus Purdue in women's lacrosse. Furthermore, the Big Ten has said that half the programming on the network will be devoted to women's sports by the third year.

For all the angst the issues caused among the Big Ten faithful, it's ironic (but illustrative) that the fiasco around the Wisconsin-Ohio State game was simply the luck of the draw. That's because the Big Ten Network gets to broadcast one home football game for each of its eleven member schools every season. Other than that one right, the Big Ten is basically at the mercy of ESPN and ABC. It gets what they don't want.

In this case, ABC took Michigan-Michigan State, ESPN showed Purdue-Penn State, and ESPN2 had Iowa-Northwestern. That left the Big Ten Network with the Wisconsin-Ohio State game. By contrast, the first two Big Ten broadcasts of Ohio State games were against Youngstown State and Akron, not the most exciting—or suspenseful—games.

Regardless of who's to blame—the Big Ten for being too greedy or the cable companies for being too cheap—the fans were annoyed with both. Viewed more broadly, I think the Big Ten Network will be a big red flag for other conferences that are thinking about following in the Big Ten's footsteps.

The only other big college conference attempting to run its own network is the Mountain West Conference. Distribution bumps have hurt it as well. As a result, other conferences are in no rush to follow the lead of these two college sports broadcasting trailblazers.

"We're watching what happens with the Big Ten Network," ACC Commissioner John Swofford told Street & Smith's *Sports Business Journal* in a November 2007 profile. "Our contracts run through 2010–11 in both football and basketball. They're separate contracts but they sync with each other chronologically. And so we've got several years to take a look at that. We're constantly evaluating the future of our television contracts and the best ways of distribution. So, what the Big Ten and the Mountain West and the NFL Network have done is of interest to us.

"The luxury we have right now is time," Swofford continued. "Sometimes you want to be out front with things. Other times you want to have the opportunity to evaluate what's happening and take a look at what it would mean to your particular situation. In this case, I think we're going to be well-served by being able to sit back and watch for a year or two how these things develop and then make a determination as to what it can mean to the ACC."

High School Football on TV

The other issue that was getting a lot of ink in 2007 was a marked increase in the broadcasting of high school football games. To truly understand the economic, social, and cultural impact of big-time college sports, you have to look at what it's doing to kids in high school and junior high.

An August 31, 2007, column by the *Houston Chronicle*'s David Barron asked readers what they'd rather watch: "A meaningless NFL exhibition game on KTRK (Ch. 13), or the most highly touted high school season opener in recent memory on FSN Houston?"

"It was an unusual choice for this time of year," Barron wrote, "but it's about to become more common," on local cable and nationwide on ESPN.

He went on to note that televising high school sports strikes some as a slippery slope. There was no such conflict for Charles Breithaupt, athletic director of the University Interscholastic League, which oversees high school sports in Texas.

"Someone is going to be on TV, and it might as well be our kids," Breithaupt told the Associated Press. "As long as we continue to protect the Friday night experience, our membership continues to be OK with it. Everybody wants to be on TV, and I can't blame them for that."

Everybody wants to be on TV. That's an understatement.

Again, I think the growth of high school sports programming is illustrative of how the money and fame of big-time college athletics (and, yes, the pros) has a reach well beyond the campus quad. It's particularly strong with young athletes, who today mimic their favorite college players as much as the pros. And it's mostly because of the aura of celebrity that twenty-four-hour sports television coverage has bestowed on kids who are supposed to be students first and athletes second.

Thanks to sports television, impressionable young kids can see—live— all the seminal moments in the careers of their favorite college athletes. The McDonald's All-American Tournament, which features the best high school senior basketball players, is broadcast live. So, too, are the tournament's shooting skills and dunking contests, which are nothing more than a chance for these kids to show off. Other high school and college TV fare includes live coverage of football and basketball signing day, the Heisman Trophy banquet, the NFL Combine and, of course, the NFL Draft.

This sort of fame and intense media focus was once the sole domain of pro athletes. Now it's accorded to players who haven't even gone to their senior prom. There's absolutely no sign that anyone is going to stand up and say "Stop." And the age at which these kids are singled out and highlighted is getting younger and younger. Later on, you'll read about the Amateur Athletic Union annual summer basketball tournament in Walt Disney World that regularly features elite teams of nine-year-olds. But we're getting ahead of ourselves.

Although the high school broadcast trend is disturbing, it's still in its infancy. The ultimate events at which the commercial development of college athletics is on full display are the college bowl games.

6 HOW MUCH DOES THAT STADIUM REALLY COST?

Going into 2009, one of the big economic concerns regarding college athletics was the so-called "facilities arms race." College presidents, endowment administrators, coaches, and the NCAA worried that colleges and universities were getting caught up in an escalating contest to see who could build the biggest, most-lavish football stadiums, basketball arenas, training facilities, and student-athlete tutoring centers. Even with the economic downturn, projects that had been planned—and funded—a few years before were continuing apace.

"You don't have to be an economist to know there's an arms race going on," said Michael Granoff, a professor of accounting at the University of Texas, which, at $107 million, has the second-highest athletic budget in all of college sports and is challenging Ohio State for the number one ranking. "Just look at what's being spent for practice facilities, facilities for non-revenue sports, and so on."

There's no doubt that schools across the country are building bigger, newer, and more opulent athletic facilities that rival those of professional sports franchises. But to me the more important question is, "Does it matter?"

What is the real impact of this facilities arms race on the overall financial health of the university? Is it jeopardizing academics for the sake of athletics? This is what we'll look at in this chapter. And, as with many of the issues surrounding big-time college athletics, the answers are not simple.

TINY ADRIAN COLLEGE ENTERS THE FRAY

Much of the debate about the facilities arms race has been around the traditional big-bucks programs: Penn State, Ohio State, Michigan, Oregon. But to understand how widespread the so-called "facilities arms race" has become, all you have to know is that even tiny Adrian College has joined the fray. In November 2005, Adrian, a 1,300-student, Division III school about an hour outside of Detroit, announced that it was going to build a 2,500-seat, $6.5 million outdoor stadium. While it wasn't akin to the construction of the 80,000-seat Yale Bowl in 1914, it was a significant undertaking for a school that size.

Adrian College's Multi-Sport Performance Stadium (who says naming rights are all bad?) opened on September 9, 2006, part of the school's alumni weekend celebration. It's pretty basic. It has synthetic turf, stadium lighting, a fully wired press box, and a student section in one end zone. The football field is ringed by an eight-lane, all-weather running track. There's also a steeplechase pit and a jumping and throwing area. A removable plastic bubble covers one half of the field during the winter months and is heated to accommodate indoor sports.

Adrian, which plays in the inconsequential Michigan Intercollegiate Athletic Association, couldn't find anyone to buy the naming rights for the new stadium, so the funds were raised through the college's development office. An alumnus, James F. Thomas ('84), did donate the money for an alumni picnic pavilion that hosts pregame tailgate parties.

The stadium is a component of the first of two phases of development being initiated by Adrian College president Jeffrey Docking. Renaissance I focused on athletic facilities, residence halls, and extracurricular life. Renaissance II focused on academics. I think it speaks volumes about Adrian and the broader issue that the athletic facilities were built first, and the academic buildings second.

In a press release announcing the board of trustees' approval to build the new stadium, the school said, "It is anticipated that the new track and stadium will boost the campus atmosphere and school spirit, and will help the College enroll more student-athletes."

"This marks the beginning of great things for Adrian College," said President Docking. "These changes will put us in stride with the ever-increasing pace of higher education, and will provide our students with an excellence of experience that they can expect from Adrian College."

Before building the stadium, the Adrian College football team was bused across town to play its home games at Maple Stadium, named for the high school team that also plays there. When the new stadium opened in 2006, it marked the first time that the football team had played on campus since the late 1950s.

"It won't be long until our teams will be playing at home, at their own facilities," Rick Creehan, executive vice president for enrollment and head of the project, said in a school press release touting the project. "Imagine having these events right on campus, where it's a short walk for students to cheer on their classmates and have a great time."

"It would be great to have more students out to support us, and that would happen if we were right on campus," said Taz Wallace, an All-American middle linebacker at Adrian. "And I think it will improve the kinds of students we can get."

And that's exactly what happened. According to a report in the April 23, 2007, *Detroit News*, freshman applications to Adrian more than doubled, and the student body grew 20 percent in one year at a time when private colleges in Michigan averaged a 2.5 percent annual increase.

Adrian College now has twenty-three NCAA varsity teams and plans to add four more teams over the next few years, which would surpass the programs offered at Michigan State and the University of Michigan.

"We can offer something to the kids who can't play for the University of Michigan," said Creehan. "You have to have a carrot to dangle in front of (students) that went beyond just the academic experience, and we chose extracurricular activities to invest in."

Of course, that's the justification that's given for the entire athletic department on college campuses across the country. It's also what is fueling the current facilities-building boom. The equation most athletic directors are doing in their heads is fairly simple: bigger stadiums plus luxury amenities equals wealthier boosters and increased revenues.

It's an economic formula that is mostly working. Furthermore, while many athletic departments carry debt, for the most part it is serviceable debt.

ATHLETICS VERSUS ACADEMICS?

So is the so-called facilities arms race really a crisis? I don't think it is.

Although clearly there's evidence that we are in the middle of a college stadium-building boom, there's also evidence that there's a facilities arms race going on in terms of academic buildings at colleges and universities across the country. Many blame this building boom for the rising cost of tuition.

So what's worse? Going into debt to build a better biology lab or a bigger library, paid for by tuition increases that are far outpacing inflation, or using the revenues from successful football and basketball programs to build new stadiums and arenas that pay for themselves through personal seat licenses, luxury suites, and a stadium club?

A 2005 study by two Washington economists that was commissioned by the NCAA concluded that athletic capital costs account for only a small proportion of overall university spending. They noted that annual capital costs at D-I athletic departments are about $24 million, just below the average operating budget, which is $27 million. In other words, most of these projects are reasonably within the operating budgets of the average athletic department. Furthermore, many are funding themselves, through increased revenues, alumni donations, and modest debt that is far from crippling.

"The inclusion of capital costs does not change the result that athletics are a small share of institutional spending," said NCAA president Myles Brand in a written statement touting the study. "However, the magnitude of these costs is a sign that they should be closely monitored and used as a tool by college presidents, boards, and athletics directors to make informed decisions about future investments."

The study did find that there was evidence of a building boom in D-I football that was feeding off itself within competitive conferences such as the SEC, Big Ten, and Pac-10. It said that an increase in seating capacity at one stadium usually resulted in increased seating at rival institutions. For evidence of this, you need look no further than the Big Ten.

BIG TEN BUILDING BOOM

Penn State completed a renovation of Beaver Stadium in 2001 that increased seating from about 93,000 to more than 107,000, making it the second-biggest facility in college sports. The project included the addition of a 10,000-seat upper deck, a new video scoreboard, sixty luxury suites, 4,000 club seats, and new restrooms and concessions.

In 2005, the University of Wisconsin completed a four-year, $110 million renovation of historic Camp Randall, the former Civil War training ground where the Badgers have played football since 1917. The facelift increased seating from 76,129 to 80,321, and added seventy-two suites, 337 club seats, and 590 varsity indoor seats. Wisconsin also added the five-story Kellner Hall office building, from which Athletic Director Barry Alvarez oversees his empire. The building is home to the Athletic Operations Building, the football offices, new visiting team lockers, the Camp Randall Media Room, and renovations and upgrades to the press box.

In 2008, the University of Michigan completed a $226 million renovation of Michigan Stadium. The project added 83 luxury suites that lease for as much as $85,000 a year, added 3,200 club seats, and increased general seating capacity by 1,000 to 108,251. Sixty miles up the road in Lansing, Michigan State completed a $64 million renovation of Spartan Stadium in 2005 that added 3,000 seats and twenty-four luxury suites, bringing capacity to 75,005.

Ohio State, the richest college athletic program in the country, with an annual budget of about $110 million, has gone on the biggest building boom of all. Over the past few years, Ohio State has built the $116 million Jerome Schottenstein Center for basketball and hockey. It completed a $194 million renovation of "The Horse Shoe" that increased capacity for football games to 105,000 screaming Buckeye fans. Ohio State also has a new baseball stadium; a new track, soccer, and lacrosse stadium; a new $4 million aquatics center; and a new $6 million boathouse for its crew team. The university also has renovated existing facilities for gymnastics, wrestling, fencing, softball, and tennis. One of Ohio State's two championship golf courses was recently redone by noted alum Jack Nicklaus.

All this capital improvement has left Ohio State's Athletic Department with debt of about $200 million, with annual debt service of about $17 million. While that sounds like a lot, think about it in the context of your own life. If you make $100,000 a year, would anyone think you were crazy to have mortgage payments of $17,000 a year on a $200,000 home loan?

Like most collegiate athletic bills, Ohio State's capital improvement debt is primarily being paid by the football and basketball teams, the school's two biggest revenue-generating sports. For instance, the stadium renovation is being paid off through a $6 surcharge on football tickets that no one seems to mind, as well as increased luxury revenue from eighty-two new suites and 5,000 club seats.

"I don't have a great need to defend Ohio State," said Dan Fulks, a Transylvania University accounting professor who analyzes athletic finances for the NCAA. "But there's no other unit on campus that has the potential to pay its own debts. You build a new biology lab, and that has to be paid for out of tuition or somewhere. If you're generating over $100 million in revenue from athletics, you have the capability of paying it off yourself."

Lessening the concern—at least in my eyes—over Ohio State's building boom is the fact that at the same time the school was paying off its $200 million athletics debt, it was giving about $3 million a year in surplus revenue to the college's general fund. Of course, as I've mentioned before, schools like Ohio State are the exception, not the rule. As I noted in earlier chapters, there are only about a half dozen athletic departments in the country that truly generate a surplus. The rest rely on student fees, alumni endowments, and other donations to stay in the black. But the fact remains that these capital improvements, no matter how big and extravagant, are not breaking the bank.

Andy Geiger, the former athletic director at Ohio State, is quick to point out that the untold story on college campuses is not the facilities arms race in athletics, but the one in the general college.

"Universities build new facilities in all areas possible in order to compete," he said. "This is especially true in research institutions. I don't think athletics does this sort of thing more than medicine or other parts of the university."

ACADEMIC BUILDINGS, TOO

Geiger has a point. A number of studies from the public and private sector blame the rising cost of tuition on a building boom on campuses across the country. Brown, Cal Tech, Columbia, Dartmouth, Johns Hopkins, and MIT are all in the $1 billion club in terms of capital campaigns. And given the low priority of athletics on their campuses, it's fair to say that the money isn't going to build new stadiums and plush locker rooms.

Johns Hopkins, which, in terms of athletics, is known for its lacrosse team but little else, hoped to raise $3.2 billion by the end of 2008. Some see the Johns Hopkins capital campaign, up from a stated goal of $2 billion in 2007, as a response to capital campaigns at Columbia, Cornell, and Stanford, all of which hoped to raise $4 billion each.

"We really aren't competing with each other," Michael C. Eicher, Johns Hopkins' vice president for development, told the *Baltimore Sun.* "It's about the real needs in the world."

There is some genuine concern that the facilities arms race in athletics is taking money away from academia. After all, there are only so many alumni with only so much to give. There is some evidence of this.

According to the *Chronicle of Higher Education,* athletics departments and booster clubs raised more than $1.2 billion in 2006–7. Between 2002 and 2007, colleges in the nation's six premier athletics conferences raised more than $3.9 billion for capital expenditures alone. Over the next few years, premier D-I programs hope to raise another $2.5 billion. Some programs have seen donations more than triple over the past decade.

"The sports fund-raising success has come at a cost," the *Chronicle* said in an October 2007 article. "While donations to the country's 119 largest athletics departments have risen significantly in recent years, overall giving to those colleges has stayed relatively flat."

Indeed, in 1998 athletics gifts accounted for 14.7 percent of all contributions. By 2003, the figure had risen to 26 percent.

"There's a fear among faculty members that there is a discrete amount of money that alums and non-alums are willing to commit," Dennis R. Howard, a professor of business at the University of Oregon, told the *Chronicle*.

He should know. Oregon, in many ways, is at the center of the facilities arms race debate. In 2007, noted alumnus Phil Knight, founder of Nike, donated $100 million to the athletic department, not the business school.

"The more the athletic program gets, the less there is to support the academic programs," Howard said.

I'm not sure that's right. As I detailed earlier, academic donations are on the rise. They're just not growing as fast as athletic contributions. Without hard evidence over a long period of time, it's a leap to say that the one is growing at the expense of the other. Furthermore, despite the rise in athletic spending, elite academic institutions seem to have no problem asking (and getting) alumni to donate $4 billion for general campus capital improvements.

It's also important to reiterate one other point here. Although athletic departments are building lavish new facilities that are paying for themselves, very few are generating a profit. That's a common misconception when it comes to the economics of college athletics. A lot of people see a big stadium with naming rights, luxury boxes, suites, a fancy club level, and a multimillion-dollar scoreboard, and assume that it generates huge piles of cash for the athletic department. That's rarely the case. The best example of this misperception is the University of North Dakota.

THE RALPH

In Grand Forks, North Dakota, which a friend joked is "an hour north of Fargo and fifteen minutes south of the Arctic Circle," the premier D-I sport is hockey. The Fighting Sioux have one of the most storied programs in all of college hockey. The school has won seven national championships and eleven Western Collegiate Athletic Association championships.

Since 2001, the Fighting Sioux have played their games in the Ralph Englestadt Arena. The facility is a $100 million gift from Englestadt, who grew up in nearby Thief River Falls, Minnesota, played goalie for the Sioux for two years, and made a fortune in construction and Las Vegas gaming. If any facility defines "plush" in college sports, this is it.

There are no bleachers in the arena. Each of the 11,500 seats is padded Sioux green leather with cherry wood armrests. Above center ice is a $2 million, thirty-thousand-pound Daktronics scoreboard with eight video screens. The fascia of the upper deck is an LCD video screen measuring nine hundred feet long and three feet high that wraps all the way around the arena. In addition to the main rink, there is an Olympic-size practice rink.

The Sioux training room is equally plush. The sauna is made of imported Norwegian teak wood. The lockers are rich cherry wood, and the floor is marble. The hot tub can accommodate almost the entire twenty-man team. On the serious side, there's an in-house X-ray room, as well as a $75,000 underwater treadmill that includes underwater cameras to monitor a player's rehabilitation regimen. The 10,000-square-foot weight room has ten platforms with ten power stations, twenty-four weight machines, thirty circuit machines, and thirty aerobic pieces. There's also an 1,800-square-foot spring-mounted floor for plyometric workouts.

Most people think that "The Ralph," as it's called, is a cash cow for North Dakota. It is, but not in the way you'd think. While Englestadt paid for all the construction and set up an endowment, 2006 marked the first time that The Ralph, which is privately held and leased to the university for $1 a year, sent a check to the university.

Part of the reason is that profits from The Ralph, which also hosts concerts and trade shows, were used to build the four-thousand-seat Betty Englestadt Sioux Center, where the women's volleyball and men's basketball teams play games.

"The Betty Englestadt Center was built and financed with the profits from The Ralph," said Phil Harmeson, North Dakota's vice president for general administration. "That was not a new $7 million gift," he said. "There's another $4 million in equipment in the building. So, in broad numbers, the profits from The Ralph are being used to service an $11 million debt."

And then there's the actual operating expenses of The Ralph, which run about $3 million a year. Hockey tickets cost $25. Of those 11,500 seats, 2,200 are set aside for students. So every hockey game generates about $232,500 in ticket revenue. In 2007–8, the Sioux had twenty home games, which generated $4.6 million in revenue.

Total athletic department revenue for 2006–7 was $11.1 million, Harmeson said. Total athletic expenses were $10.9 million. Part of that $11.1 million revenue was the first-ever surplus payment from The Ralph, totaling about $350,000. So without the modest profit of The Ralph, North Dakota, even with a debt-free $100 million hockey arena that is the envy of every other college hockey program in the country, would have been in the red. Clearly a different picture than most fans and critics imagine.

I did point out to Harmeson that The Ralph does have an immeasurable economic value to North Dakota. Without it, the school would have built some sort of facility for the hockey team. It may not have been the $100 million palace that alumnus Ralph Englestadt chose to build. But it would have been comparable to, say, the 10,000-seat Mariucci Arena that opened on the University of Minnesota campus in 1993, or the 6,300-seat Agganis Arena at Boston University, part of the $225 million John Hancock Student Village. Either way, in a fair accounting of the North Dakota Athletic Department, The Ralph should count as a fairly big debit.

The other controversy surrounding the University of North Dakota hockey team has been its Fighting Sioux nickname. The issue came to a head in August 2005 when the NCAA listed UND among eighteen schools with mascots or nicknames that were considered "hostile or abusive." To pressure these schools to change their names, the NCAA said that the teams couldn't host NCAA-sanctioned playoffs or use the nicknames in postseason play. Some schools in the Western Collegiate Hockey Association pressured North Dakota, as well. St. Cloud (Minnesota) State University president Roy Saigo, a Japanese-American who was imprisoned during World War II, told North Dakota that they could not wear the uniforms that featured the colorful Fighting Sioux Indianhead logo that, ironically, was designed by a Sioux artist. Instead, the team wore jerseys that simply read "North Dakota." Susan Ihne, the controversial editor at the Gannett-owned

St. Cloud Times, also issued an edict to her sports department, forbidding them to use the proper names of teams—college or professional—with offensive team names. So all of the stories in the *St. Cloud Times* simply referred to the Sioux as "the North Dakota hockey team" or simply "North Dakota."

The University of Wisconsin, whose moniker during the Cold War was "Moscow on the Mendota," because of its harsh left-wing tilt, also said it would refuse to play games in North Dakota.

At the center of the debate was Ralph Englestadt himself. He argued that the Sioux nickname was a source of pride, not ridicule. It embodied the warrior spirit of the Sioux people. That got him nowhere with critics. Outside of North Dakota, he was lambasted in the media. While many articles mentioned his $100 million donation to the school, they also focused on his car collection at the Imperial Palace Hotel and Casino in Las Vegas, which featured one of Hitler's staff cars. The implication was that he was some sort of Nazi because he refused to change the nickname. Although there was apparently some validity to the claim—the Nevada Gaming Commission fined him $1.5 million for "glorifying Hitler"—it had nothing to do with the Sioux nickname debate.

Ralph didn't help matters. He stuck a thumb in the eye of the protesters by having an estimated twelve thousand Sioux Indianhead logos designed into the arena. They're etched into the back of every seat, and a giant Sioux Indianhead logo is carved into the Italian marble entryways. And he purposely built the arena on private property and leased it to the university for $1 a year so that protestors couldn't gather outside the arena. Because it's private property, the closest they can get to the entrance is a few hundred yards.

After a round of lawsuits and lots of angst, the NCAA punted in late 2007. It said that North Dakota had three years to bring Sioux tribal leaders on board or come up with another nickname. That's interesting, because the split among the Sioux over the nickname mirrors a similar split in the Seminole tribes, but Florida State was given a pass by the NCAA.

What makes this all the worse is the fact that North Dakota has some of the most extensive—and endowed—Native-American programs in the country. For instance, an estimated 20 percent of all Native-American doctors and dentists are North Dakota grads. Many of them went to school because North Dakota offers full-ride need-based and academic scholarships.

"We have about 450 Native-American students, the highest percentage of Native-American students in any population in the country," Harmeson said. "We also have the largest array of programs specifically for Native-Americans. We offer everything from business to nursing to medicine to law to aerospace. Virtually all of our signature programs have done very well in crafting programs and support programs to not only educate Native Americans, but to train them to go back and help their communities, some of which remain very challenged."

Harmeson said that if you walk into almost any Native-American school in North Dakota and northern Minnesota, the vast majority of teachers are UND grads. Many of the administrators are, also.

"Go into a tribal hospital or clinic, and the majority are UND graduates, as well," he said.

What's more, in 2007 the Englestadt family made a $10 million donation to North Dakota.

"A significant portion is dedicated to qualifying Native-American students," Harmeson said.

None of this seemed to matter to Englestadt's critics.

"On a campus where there are Indian students, it's offensive to them," said Jim McKenzie, chairman of the English Department. He said he didn't know a single member of the Arts and Sciences faculty who would step inside Ralph Englestadt Arena.

Maybe he should talk to junior forward T. J. Oshie, who's part Ojibwe, or Chippewa.

"The Fighting Sioux name is part of our team," said the Minnesota Indian Education Association's male athlete of 2005. "You hear us say that we're going to play 'Fighting Sioux hockey.' Not only is that working hard and scoring goals, it's also playing with pride. It's part of our tradition here. It would really be sad to see it go away."

I agree.

Although these increasingly upscale stadiums and arenas aren't turning huge profits for college athletic departments, not many fans seem to be complaining about their price tags. For instance, there was little outcry when Ohio State raised ticket prices $6 to pay for the renovation of The Horse Shoe.

One exception to the luxury box trend is Notre Dame, which "made a conscious decision not to enter into the skybox business because it is a professional sports concept," said associate athletic director John Heisler.

What opposition there is to these new sports palaces is coming from a familiar foe: academia. Faculty members and some administrators look at these luxurious, multimillion-dollar sports palaces and think, "If only the Chemistry Department had that money."

BIG HOUSE BROU-HA-HA

One of the angriest faculties in America when it comes to college athletics is the University of Michigan. And the renovation of Michigan Stadium did not go unchallenged.

As I mentioned, Michigan's $226 million renovation of "The Big House" put eighty-three luxury boxes where mostly bleachers have been since the stadium opened in 1927. Luxury box revenue financed most of it. With the school's general fund off the hook for the cost, defenders were quick to point out that the $226 million savings is equal to about ten thousand full academic scholarships. If you price the academic aid at in-state rates, it's equal to thirty thousand free rides. Even if you don't agree with that mathematical calculation, the economics of the new stadium are pretty compelling.

In 2005, Michigan started selling personal seat licenses for prime locations in the Big House and sold out immediately. More important, thanks to PSLs and other luxury amenities, Michigan football is in the black for the first time in years.

"When I came in six years ago, we had a deficit of $5 million," said Athletic Director Bill Martin. "I do have to pay for updating Michigan Stadium, and there is no other economic model that I know of to do it."

That argument didn't sit well with a group of vocal critics—mostly faculty and alumni who aren't fans of the football team—who operated under the rubric "Save the Big House." They fought the renovation every step of the way and, like the alumni who tried to point out the brutality of college football at the turn of the 20th century, were thwarted at almost every turn. Their chief spokesman was John Pollack, son of a University of Michigan professor and a former speechwriter for President Bill Clinton.

Pollack and his supporters started out with a classic class-warfare argument.

"To enshrine wealth and power in glass and steel at the leading public institution totally undermines the values of the university itself," Pollack told the *New York Times* in a 2007 interview. "You are taking the classic football stadium in America and turning it into every NFL venue."

Michigan Stadium, Pollack argued, is one of the great public spaces in America, akin to Central Park. And it knows no class. It is, he said, "a place where autoworkers and millionaires can come together to cheer on their team."

Furthermore, Ann Arbor doesn't have to engage in the facilities arms race.

"Michigan doesn't need to keep up with the Joneses," Pollack said. "We are the Joneses."

When the egalitarianism argument didn't work, Pollack and his cabal got the Education Department to investigate the project for violating the Americans with Disabilities Act.

"Clearly, the University of Michican felt it is more important to accommodate millionaires in luxury boxes than it is to guarantee equal access to the stadium for disabled fans," said the "Save the Big House" group.

Pollack claimed that the administration ignored a petition signed by more than six hundred faculty members and staffers, as well as the Senate Assembly. The university was also sued by the Michigan chapter of the Paralyzed Veterans of America.

"It's outrageous," said Richard Bernstein, the group's lawyer. "This case goes to the heart and soul of the Americans with Disabilities Act."

Michigan argued that the stadium, which was built in 1927, was being repaired, not renovated. Thus, it was not subject to a 1990 law that covers disabled persons.

In addition to the ADA issue, Pollack and his supporters argued that erecting two large buildings for luxury suites above the Michigan Stadium bowl, which is below ground, would, among other things, block out the sun and change the architectural flavor of the place.

Aesthetics and ADA compliance aside, Michigan was easily able to afford to renovate the Big House. It has an $87 million athletic budget and turned a $17 million profit in 2006. Even in noncompetitive years—like the one that just forced out long-time coach Lloyd Carr—loyal fans still fill the Big House every Saturday. The same is true for Notre Dame, which in 2007 had one of its worst seasons in history but still generates $60 million a year just from football, more than any other program in the country. But the economics of the arms race are causing some schools that may—or may not—be able to afford a big stadium to build one anyway.

Good cases in point are Florida International University, Central Florida, and the University of South Florida, all of which moved up to Division I in 2007. Central Florida, which had $7.8 million in football revenue in 2006 and has yet to break even, is spending $54 million to build 45,000-seat Bright House Networks Stadium.

Florida International University has gotten the go-ahead for a $31 million renovation of its stadium that will add 10,500 new seats, 1,400 club seats, fourteen luxury suites, a wraparound concourse, a new video scoreboard, and a stadium club.

"This will be a crown jewel for the University," said Athletic Director Pete Garcia. "It's going to be a student complex center and also our stadium. This is going to be the center of campus eventually, when it's finished and finalized."

In 2007, students paid $20 per semester in athletic fees. The Athletic Department proposed to increase the fee by $1.39 per credit hour to pay for the renovation. That would generate about $1.1 million a year in revenue for the Athletic Department. About $655,000 of that would go toward paying back the bonds, while the rest will be used for marketing athletics and ticket sales.

While these two projects may sound like pretty big economic gambles for two commuter schools, they're taking their cues from the University of South Florida. In 2007, the school's Top 25 ranking boosted football attendance by 69 percent over the previous season. The South Florida Bulls averaged 51,088 fans for each of four home games at Raymond James Stadium in Tampa in 2007, compared with 30,222 in 2006.

"Most institutions look at what attracts alumni, what makes them contribute," Central Florida athletic director Keith Tribble told the *New York Times* in an October 28, 2007, story titled "SKYBOX U."

"Without fail, it all comes back to football," he said. "Most of the great institutions in the country are tied to the hip with athletics."

"The only way they can fill their stadiums is to build winning teams— and to continue winning, year after year," wrote *New York Times* business reporter Joe Nocera. "They have jumped on a treadmill that they now can't afford to get off."

So why do they do it? he asked.

"Partly because they're in Florida, perhaps the most football-mad state in the country," he said. "Partly because football is believed to be the best single marketing and advertising program any university can have."

They're not alone. Old Dominion University in Norfolk, Virginia, is resurrecting its football program after it was dormant for sixty-seven years. The school is spending $25 million to renovate seventy-two-year-old Foreman Field in Norfolk. A new four-story building in the stadium's south end zone will contain twenty-four suites and one hundred four-seat loge boxes. Revenue from the premium seating will help pay for construction and financially support Old Dominion's move in 2009 into the NCAA Football Championship Subdivision, formerly known as I-AA.

NAMING RIGHTS

Another athletic revenue-generating trend that was garnering headlines in 2007 was naming rights. Of the 119 largest college football stadiums in America, only three have sold names to corporations: Papa John's Pizza at the University of Louisville, SBC Communications Stadium at Texas Tech, and the Carrier (Heating and Air Conditioning) Dome at Syracuse. The Univesity of Minnesota, cash-strapped for money for a new on-campus stadium, is close to becoming the fourth such school—and first in the Big Ten—to sell stadium naming rights.

For twenty years the Gophers have played their home games in the cavernous Metrodome, a 62,000-seat indoor stadium that sells out for the NFL's Minnesota Vikings but is usually only half full for Gopher college football games. The exceptions are when the Gophers play Wisconsin or Iowa, schools that are close enough for their traveling boosters.

Enter TCF Financial. The Minneapolis bank has agreed to put up $35 million to help with construction of the new $250 million open-air, on-campus stadium (the state and university will pay the rest). The bank even agreed to give up traditional naming rights because older alumni insisted that the new facility be called "Memorial Stadium," the name of the old stadium that memorialized soldiers from World War I. Under the current plan, it would be called "TCF Field at Memorial Stadium."

I don't think naming rights is a trend that's going to explode anytime soon. Unlike with pro teams, there's too much tradition at many of these schools. Besides, if schools such as Penn State, Wisconsin, and Ohio State were going to sell naming rights, they would have done it during this last round of renovations.

What is interesting about the TCF deal in Minnesota is what's not being reported. In addition to funding for the stadium, TCF will give the University of Minnesota another $10 million for purely academic scholarships in biosciences and genetic engineering. In exchange, TCF will get some premium placement on campus for its ATM machines.

This is not unusual. Sponsorships often come with strings attached. It's just that the fine print is rarely reported. So, like Notre Dame's television money, the TCF money that Minnesota will get will go to something other than academics.

Of course, the athletic arms race isn't limited to just stadiums. It has spilled over into practice facilities, as well. In October 2007, the University of Louisville opened the Yum Center, its new college basketball practice facility. The $15.2 million, 61,000-square-foot building is a big part of basketball coach Rick Pitino's plan to bridge the gap between Freedom Hall, the off-campus arena where the Cardinals play their home basketball games, and a new downtown arena where Louisville will be the primary tenant starting in 2010. Built along Interstate 64, which runs along the east side of campus, the Yum Center's two-story glass wall features a huge Cardinal logo that can easily be seen from the highway.

Not to be outdone, the University of Kentucky recently opened the Joe Craft Center, which at 93,000 square feet and $30 million is the most expensive basketball practice facility in Division I.

Coach Bob Huggins and his staff from West Virginia visited both places. The Mountaineers expect to spend up to $20 million to develop a privately financed practice facility next to WVA Coliseum.

So what's the lesson to be learned from all this? I think University of Virginia Athletic Director Jon Oliver sums it up nicely. He oversaw the construction of the school's new $130 million John Paul Jones Arena.

Oliver told *Sports Business Journal* that the arena has already helped the men's basketball team recruit players.

"The last 10 years, we really weren't on anybody's final list that was a top 20 player," he said. "Now . . . of the top 15 players in the next recruiting class, we're on every one of their lists."

Oliver said the school has sold all twenty suites in the arena, but that he had one regret.

"If I had to do it all over again," he said, "I would have built more suites."

COACHES CASH IN, TOO

Most people have two fundamental questions when it comes to the ever-rising salaries of college coaches: Do they make more than the university president, and do they earn it? The answer to both may surprise you.

A good example of a typical D-I coach's salary is that of Auburn University head football coach Tommy Tuberville, who left the school in December 2008. His total compensation was over $2 million a year, whereas President Jay Gogue earns just $450,000. Critics would look at that and decry the fact that the football coach makes four times as much as the college president. But in terms of what the university has to shell out, the president actually makes twice as much as the coach.

Yes, Tuberville earned more than $2 million a year, but only $235,000 came directly out of the Auburn coffers. The vast majority of Tuberville's salary came from the $51.3 million multimedia and marketing rights contract that Auburn has with ISP Sports. Thanks to the new deal, in 2008 Auburn saw a 138 percent increase in rights fees, earning $5.7 million a year. Tuberville was paid $1.5 million as part of the deal, so ISP Sports was actually paying three-quarters of Tuberville's $2 million annual salary.

IT'S THE PERKS, NOT THE PAY

Tuberville wasn't alone. On average, only about 25 percent of a big-time college coach's full compensation comes in the form of salary. The rest comes from television and apparel contracts, endorsements, and other side deals. Other coaching perks often include a free car, an expense account, or a country club membership, all of which are often donated by boosters (and qualify as a tax write-off because it's for "education").

Despite this fact, some people are still critical of coaches' salaries.

"Since the players don't get paid, you can't just go out and hire the Tom Bradys of college sports," sports economist Andrew Zimbalist wrote in his book *Unpaid Professionals*. "So instead they throw money at everything else," including coaches.

"They get paid pretty much the same as coaches in the N.F.L., about $2 to $3 million," he said. "It doesn't make any sense from a normal economic point of view, because the average revenue of a top-30 college football team is about $30 million, whereas the average N.F.L. team takes in $200 million."

Schools justify the high salaries, Zimbalist said, because they "want to be able to say that they have a coach with a national reputation, someone who has sent kids off to the N.F.L."

This, of course, raises the question, "Do these high-dollar coaches really earn the money they make?"

You decide.

Tuberville and his staff earned a combined salary of about $5 million a year. Even if Auburn were footing the whole bill, those salaries accounted for about 10 percent of the school's total athletic budget of about $50 million, a major percentage of which is generated by the football program. Sticking to this simple math, Tuberville and his staff yielded a tenfold return on their salary for Auburn.

Where a top coach can really rake in the cash for his school is by taking the team to a bowl game. Because a team's travel expenses are usually covered by the bowl committee, the bulk of bowl money paid to participating schools is almost pure profit (although it is further diluted by conference revenue sharing).

On December 31, 2007, Auburn traveled to Atlanta to meet Clemson in the Chick-fil-A (formerly Peach) Bowl. Auburn's one-day payout? $2.8 million. Again, if you figure that Auburn—one way or another—was paying Tuberville's entire $5 million salary, the bowl appearance earned back half that. If you calculated Auburn's contribution to Tuberville's total compensation at just his $235,000 salary, the Chick-fil-A Bowl paid Auburn ten times what it paid Tuberville. Yes, some of it was distributed to other SEC schools because most conferences share postseason revenues. But that's a decision the presidents of the participating schools made, and one they would have to abide by regardless of who was the coach, what he was being paid, and how many bowls he went to. The fact of the matter remains that for $235,000 Auburn got a football coach who earned ten times his salary in lucrative postseason cash in 2008.

THE $4 MILLION CLUB

Other highly paid coaches offer similar financial returns to their employers. Ohio State's Jim Tressel and the University of Texas's Mack Brown are among the dozen or so football coaches who make more than $2 million a year. Oklahoma's Bob Stoops is paid a guaranteed $3 million a year, and Alabama's Nick Saban topped them all in 2007 when he left the Miami Dolphins and signed an eight-year, $32 million deal to coach in Tuscaloosa. While those numbers are eye popping, you have to compare them to the revenues that those sports (and, arguably, those coaches) generate.

Ohio State has the largest athletic budget in college sports, although Texas is closing fast. Ohio State athletics generates revenues of about $109 million a year, with the football program bringing in about $60 million. Tressel's efforts have contributed more than $10 million in postseason money over the past few years, primarily from two Bowl Championship Series appearances (though losing both times).

Texas's athletic budget is $107 million, with football accounting for about half of that. The team earned $2.1 million for appearing in the 2008 Pacific Life Holiday Bowl, and more than $17 million for playing in the 2009 Fiesta Bowl. The University of Oklahoma's athletic budget has risen from $28 million in 1999 to $62 million in 2006, with football contributing about $40 million, or two-thirds. The team also pocketed the $17.5 million per school BCS payout for playing in the 2009 National Championship game. Another $17.5 million winner was Alabama, which played in the 2008 Sugar Bowl. Its annual athletic budget is nearly $70 million, with $44 million coming from football.

So do the math. Tressel, Brown, Stoops, and Saban had combined salaries of $11 million, but their schools have easily earned more than that in postseason bowl money over the past few years.

Les Miles, whose LSU Tigers beat Ohio State in the 2008 BCS Championship Game, 38 to 24, isn't doing badly either. LSU football rakes in about $50 million a year. Under terms of his new contract, which pays him almost $3 million a year, Miles could earn an added bonus of $3.5 million.

SCHOOLS DON'T PAY

If those salaries still sound too high to justify—regardless of where the money's coming from—these coaches aren't alone. A 2006 survey of coaches' salaries by *USA Today* showed that top Division I coaches are earning on average $950,000 a year, without counting benefit packages or other perks. At least thirty-five coaches make $1 million or more, and a growing elite make more than $2 million. Again, the important factor here is that while most coaches do make more than their college president (or governor), the biggest part of a coach's compensation comes from off-campus deals. In other words, the school isn't sacrificing biology textbooks for basketballs.

Most college coaches at big-time D-I programs have lucrative television contracts, shoe and apparel deals, and other endorsements that make up the lion's share of their total compensation package. For instance, North Carolina basketball coach Roy Williams makes about $1.6 million a year, but only $260,000 of it comes in the form of salary. The school also provides him with a $25,000 expense account and a $22,000 bonus each time the team advances through the March Madness brackets, from simply making the tournament to the Elite 8. He also gets a bonus if the team's graduation rate equals that of the general student body. But the bulk of his compensation comes from off campus. Williams is being paid a $3.9 million bonus over five seasons by the Rams Club, one of the Tarheels's wealthy booster clubs. He also gets nearly $350,000 in radio and TV money and about $500,000 from Nike as part of North Carolina's all-school shoe and apparel contract.

Across campus, UNC football coach John Bunting makes about $650,000 a year. But North Carolina pays just $300,000 of that. The school pays his $260,000 salary, a $25,000-per-year expense account, and a potential $22,000 bonus for making postseason play. Bunting makes $225,000 from radio and television and $150,000 from Nike.

Coach K over at Duke makes about $1.5 million a year, with about $900,000 in the form of salary. That makes Coach K the highest-paid Duke faculty member. Surprisingly, he hasn't always held that position. Eugene McDonald made $1.2 million in salary before he retired as the head of Duke's investment arm. And Ralph Snyderman, who has also since left the university, made more than $1 million as the chancellor of Duke's health affairs.

So, do an increasing number of college coaches make $1 million or more? Absolutely. Are their salaries that far off from other faculty members? Yes. But they aren't alone.

NCAA president Myles Brand, who can always be counted on to prop up the façade that college athletics is a purely amateur endeavor, argued in a letter to Congress (defending the tax-exempt status of university athletic income) that coaches' salaries are commensurate with those of other highly paid faculty.

"There are likely to be as many as two dozen 'million dollar faculty' members on each of these [Division I-A] campuses who earn a relatively small salary from the institution with the balance coming in the form of clinical and private practices, patent royalties, consulting contracts, books, speaking engagements and other sources," Brand wrote. "It should be noted, however, that faculty members have the protection of tenure while coaches are employed at will and can be dismissed for lackluster win-loss records or the inappropriate behavior of 18- to 22-year olds."

Brand's right about the risks, but wrong about faculty compensation.

The fear of every college coach and athletic director isn't an abysmal won-loss record. It's the fact that their careers can be ruined by one stupid nineteen-year-old kid who decides to have too much to drink on a Friday night and gets a DUI or roughs up his cheerleader girlfriend. These—and myriad other stupid decisions by these kids—can ruin a coach's career in an instant. And there's not a thing he can do about it.

But Brand is wrong about the million-dollar faculty members. They're a statistical anomaly. A rarity. Just like the college coaches who make $1 million or more. Yes, their numbers are rising, but they're still the exception, not the rule. The fact that many people probably believe that every college coach makes a million dollars is just another example of the distortions and misconceptions that are caused by a sports media that focuses primarily on the two most lucrative college sports—football and basketball—and often forgets about the women's volleyball coach who makes $30,000 a year (or less). It seems like there are more million-dollar coaches because every time one of them breaks into that elite category, we read about them for months on end.

According to Gary R. Roberts, deputy dean of Tulane University's law school and director of its sports law program, the only professors making seven-figure salaries are at a handful of elite medical schools. And even they are not good examples, he argues, because they really aren't classroom faculty in the same sense as other teachers.

According to the American Association of University Professors, the average faculty salary in 2005–6 was $100,000 at public doctoral research universities and $130,000 at private doctoral institutions. For example, UCLA pays its full-time professors about $100,000 a year. Meanwhile, head football coach Karl Dorrell, who was released at the end of the 2007 season, had a base salary of $181,000 and total compensation of $881,000, according to *USA Today* figures. He was replaced by Rick Neuheisel, who was the MVP quarterback for UCLA in the 1984 Rose Bowl. He's making about $1.25 million a year at UCLA.

Neuheisel is interesting because he's another example of how coaches can recycle themselves, even after being fired. In 2005, Neuheisel reached a $4.5 million settlement with the University of Washington and the NCAA as part of a wrongful termination suit he filed. Neuheisel was fired in 2003 after he admitted betting $6,400 in an off-campus NCAA March Madness pool. For the record: he won $17,000. He also ran into trouble while he was the coach at Colorado. The school was placed on two years' probation for what the NCAA called secondary—meaning minor—recruiting violations, mostly involving improper contact with recruits.

Despite the fact that the coaches' million-dollar club is still a relatively small group, and a major part of their compensation comes from outside the school, many coaches continue to come under fire for making what many believe to be hundreds of thousands, if not millions, more than the average faculty member.

"If a coach is getting five times as much as a university president and 10 or 20 times as much as an average full-time professor, that's making a statement to the student body about what's important," Zimbalist said in *Unpaid Professionals.*

I'm surprised that an economist of Zimbalist's repute is missing the core economic principle at work here. As much as it may offend our sense of righteousness and virtue, the fact of the matter is that a lot more people are interested in watching Joe Paterno coach football than they are in watching Penn State's most gifted engineering professor discuss the principles of thermodynamics. In short, it's simple demand theory.

SKEWED AVERAGE

What further muddies the coach-prof debate is the fact that the salaries of a handful of elite coaches such as USC's Peter Carroll ($2.8 million) and Alabama's Nick Saban ($4 million) skew the average. Indeed, when you mix the Notre Dames and Ohio States in with the Valparaisos and Oberlins, head football coaches make on average about $185,000, men's basketball coaches $157,500, and head women's basketball coaches $108,000. When you include all institutions, including two-year colleges, those numbers drop significantly—to $74,000 for a head football coach and $63,000 for a men's basketball coach.

"We're talking about a small percentage of football coaches in America who attain this [million-dollar] status," said Grant Teaff, executive director of the American Football Coaches Association. "The majority of coaches, like a majority of teachers, work for much less."

There's certainly no denying that the number of million-dollar coaches is on the rise. According to the *USA Today* study, at least 42 of the 119 Division I-A coaches earned $1 million or more in 2006, up from just five coaches in 1999. And then there are the coaches who fly under the radar, like Iowa's Kirk Ferentz.

Ferentz made an astonishing $4.6 million a year in guaranteed salary and bonuses. His base salary was $1.4 million, which included shoe and apparel endorsements, as well as money for a summer football camp, radio, and TV. He also received four supplemental payments of $350,000 each throughout the year, as well as a $400,000 longevity bonus. And his latest contract extension included a one-time payment of $1.4 million. If he had taken the Hawkeyes to a bowl game in 2008 that paid $1 million or more, he would have received a $75,000 bonus. He would have gotten just $25,000 if the team had gone to a bowl game that paid less than a million. There's also an incentive bonus if the team has a graduation rate of 55 percent. In July 2009, Ferentz signed a contract extension that will keep him in Iowa City through 2015. By contrast, Iowa president Sally Mason makes $450,000.

Performance incentives and other side deals like those in Ferentz's compensation package are increasingly the norm, not the exception. In 2006–7, coaches at more than eighty schools had about $23 million in on-field performance bonuses at stake. Florida's Urban Meyer pocketed $37,500 for getting the Gators to the Southeastern Conference title game; another $137,500 for winning the game and qualifying for a BCS game; $50,000 just for getting into the national title game; and another $100,000 for winning it. In short, Meyer took home $325,000 in postseason bonus money.

Maryland's Ralph Friedgen gets $50,000 a year for good behavior. I'm not making that up. If he, his coaches, and his players do not violate university student conduct or academic rules, have no arrests, nor violate any NCAA rules, he earns the bonus. Texas's Mack Brown gets $20,000 if the football team's graduation rate is at least 50 to 54 percent. The bonus rises to $100,000 if the graduation rate is 75 percent (the Division I-A average is about 70 percent).

ARE THEY WORTH IT?

While the figures in the preceding section are astounding, especially for a coach like Ferentz, you have to consider this. Going into the 2007–8 season, Division I-A schools have shared more than $900 million in bowl payouts in the past six years, according to the Football Bowl Association. Do the math on that. At the time there were thirty-two bowl games. If you have two head coaches per game and they're each making a million dollars, then the salary for bowl coaches was $64 million. Multiply that by six and you get $384 million in head coaching salaries for bowl games over that six-year period. Divide that by the more than $900 million in bowl proceeds that have been distributed, and these schools are seeing a threefold return on their money. Try getting that on Wall Street today.

In 2008–9 alone, D-I schools divided more than $200 million in bowl proceeds. Again, divide that by the $64 million that's theoretically spent on coaches' salaries, and it's again a three- to four-time return on their money. Over the next decade, schools will see more than $2 billion in bowl money. Even at the inflated rate, that's a fourfold return on their coaching investment.

"Is (Ferentz's compensation) fair?" Iowa athletic director Gary Barta asked in a 2007 interview. "I'm not going to judge that. Is it the reality across the country? Yes. We want to keep Kirk here. The marketplace drives what we pay . . . and right now the marketplace is aggressive."

Of course, a lot of the rise in coaching salaries is directly related to the rise in media money pouring into college sports. Tuberville's deal at Auburn, of which three-quarters was funded by media rights from ISP Sports, is becoming more common. And you have to remember that the money that these coaches bring in pays for a lot more than just their team's expenses.

At Texas, head football coach Mack Brown makes more than $2 million a year, but football accounted for 62 percent of the athletic department's more than $100 million in revenue. Thanks to football, Texas athletics has an initial surplus of about $42 million. That money is then used to underwrite seventeen other school sports, many of them Title IX-mandated women's sports, which don't make a penny. Given all that, is it really unfair that Mark Yudof, chancellor of the University of Texas system, make about $700,000, or about a third of what Brown makes?

Of course, many of the schools I've just talked about have a long and storied history of athletic success and repeated—and lucrative—postseason play. But even schools that are relative newcomers to the big-bucks world of college athletics and have limited success in the postseason are paying their coaches what many consider to be outrageous salaries.

A good example is Marquette University, a tiny, private Jesuit college in Milwaukee. At the start of the 2007–8 season, Tom Crean was entering his eighth year as head coach of Marquette's men's basketball team. (At the end of the 2008 season, he took the head coaching job at Indiana.)

Crean's career record at Marquette was 165-86, meaning he won 65.7 percent of his games. Despite the Jesuit's vow of poverty, he was clearly in the upper echelon of college basketball coaches, both in terms of won-loss record and salary.

According to IRS records that Marquette is required to file as a nonprofit institution, Crean made about $1.65 million a year, which included his base pay as well as compensation for basketball camps and radio and TV appearances (see Table 7.1). Marquette also put nearly $29,000 a year into his retirement plan, and in 2006 paid him $3,784 for expenses. His salary had increased markedly over the last few years. In 2002, he made about $565,000 a year, or about a third of what he made before leaving for Indiana. In 2003, his salary jumped to $776,830 and in 2004 to $1.1 million. By comparison, University of Wisconsin basketball coach Bo Ryan makes about $700,000.

In the Big East, Crean's salary was comparable to Connecticut coach Jim Calhoun, who made about $1.4 million a year. But Crean's salary at Marquette paled in comparison to Louisville Cardinals head basketball coach

TABLE 7.1

Top College Basketball Coach Incomes

Coach	School	Income
Tom Crean	Marquette	$1.65 million
Rick Pitino	Louisville	$1.64 million
Tom Izzo	Michigan State	$1.6 million
Jim Calhoun	Connecticut	$1.4 million
Mike Krzyzewski	Duke	$1.4 million
Roy Williams	North Carolina	$1.4 million
Bo Ryan	Wisconsin	$700,000
Jim Boeheim	Syracuse	$377,387
Rob Jeter	UW-Milwaukee	$300,000

Source: Author's research.

Rick Pitino. Starting in 2007–8, Pitino was set to earn a base salary of $2.25 million over the next three seasons, and then $2.5 million a year from 2010 through 2013. Pitino, who was hired in 2001, also has several deferred compensation bonuses in his contract, including a July 1, 2007, payment of $1.75 million. He can earn an extra $3.6 million if he is still coaching in March of 2010 and another $3.6 million if he completes the new contract. All told, Pitino can earn $23.2 million over the six-year life of his latest contract—and that's excluding performance bonuses. In August 2009, we of course learned that Pitino allegedly used some of that bonus money to pay a Louisville waitress to get an abortion after they had an affair. She, in turn, allegedly tried to blackmail him for $2 million.

Other highly paid college basketball coaches include Tennessee's Bruce Pearl, who agreed to a one-year contract extension for 2007–8 that paid him $1.3 million in total compensation. And every time he renews, he gets a $100,000 raise. Oregon coach Ernie Kent, who led the Ducks to the Elite Eight in the 2007 NCAA Tournament, agreed to a five-year contract extension that pays him $1 million a year through the 2011–12 season. University of Washington men's basketball coach Lorenzo Romar signed a new contract for the 2007–8 season that paid him a guaranteed $1.1 million each season, along with $200,000 in deferred compensation and another $200,000 in performance bonuses. Romar's extension gives him a contract more than double his original six-year deal, which paid him $700,000. That first contract was torn up in 2005, when the Huskies made a second consecutive NCAA Tournament appearance, and was replaced with an eight-year extension that gave him a deal worth more than $1 million annually.

Although Crean's $1.6 million salary may have seemed like a lot to the English professor making $80,000, the figures that matter most to Marquette are these: over seven seasons, Crean led Marquette to three NCAA tournament appearances, including a Final Four appearance in 2003. And that's why Marquette paid Crean so much. A Marquette biology professor may teach Cell Biology 101 to a student who finds the cure for cancer, but that won't get the school a share of the $6.1 billion that CBS recently paid for the broadcast rights to March Madness, which gets distributed to schools that make the tournament. And Marquette clearly understands that. In short, while the biology professor may be teaching students who go on to do life-saving research, the free market pays more for basketball coaches. Sad, but true.

"Seven years ago, Marquette University made a conscious decision to upgrade its athletic programs, including the recruitment of outstanding coaches, development of new facilities and, this year, the move to the Big East Conference," university spokeswoman Mary Pat Pfeil said in a statement that defended Crean's salary. "This is an investment from which the university is reaping returns . . . in the form of national media exposure, in the significant revenues generated by the men's basketball program, in the number of prospective students who become familiar with Marquette through its athletic program, in student excitement, and in the alumni and community support generated by a successful athletic program."

She's absolutely right. She's just ticked off all of the sound economic rationales for which a major university has an athletic program. March Madness and the Bowl Championship Series are a pretty efficient—and high-profile—way to tell kids in California about your school in Connecticut. If a university has a revenue-generating intercollegiate sport, with few exceptions it's either football or basketball, thanks to revenues from television, ticket sales, and suite rentals. And, of course, there are the alumni, many of whom stay connected to the university through athletics and sometimes feel compelled to give $100 or $100 million to support their favorite team.

A key component to any successful athletic program is a winning coach. And while it may seem anathema to the school's academic mission, the benefits of paying a first-rate coach a first-rate salary are evident even to the good Jesuits at Marquette.

"The university makes fair and competitive compensation a key priority in attracting high-quality faculty and staff in all areas," Pfeil said. "Salary differentiations among employment categories are, to a large degree, a function of the marketplace. College basketball is a competitive market, particularly at the Division I level. In keeping with our commitment to attract and retain the best faculty and staff, we believe Coach Crean's position is important to the university."

HOW MUCH IS ENOUGH?

Of course, for some coaches, the million-dollar salary, sneaker contracts, free car, expense account, and country club membership are not enough. Some try to bend the rules with lucrative side deals, sometimes in violation of the labyrinthine NCAA rulebook, which no one has ever read and fewer claim to fully comprehend.

In late 2007, one of the most bizarre examples involved Texas A&M football coach Dennis Franchione, who was augmenting his salary with a little side work. He was the author of a weekly newsletter about the football program called *VIP Connection*. One problem: He was selling subscriptions to boosters for $1,200 a year. Making matters worse, he sometimes discussed the status of injured players, talked specifically about promising high school recruits, and accepted outside sports-related income without the approval of the school. All no-nos in the NCAA's eyes. But he did it nonetheless, despite the fact that he was earning more than $2 million a year and had an $8 million buyout clause in his contract.

His worst transgression, many agreed, was the weekly injury report, which could be used by oddsmakers in Las Vegas. Gambling is the biggest, baddest bogeyman for the NCAA. It has reared its head more than a few times over the years, and its ill effects sometimes taint a program for decades.

"I think the NCAA will generally be concerned with the possibility of providing information to gamblers, whether knowingly or not," University of Houston compliance officer Kevin Fite said during a press conference in response to the Franchione incident. "But it's pretty hard to nail that down. He would have to know or have reason to know they were using the information for gambling."

In defending himself, Franchione said the intent of the insider e-mail newsletter was to help offset the cost of running his personal Web site, www.coachfran.com. Franchione said the $1,200 annual payments from a dozen or so boosters went directly to the company that maintains his Web site. Unfortunately, that's in violation of Section 2.3 of his contract, which states that Franchione is prohibited from receiving any money or benefits or gratuity whatsoever from any university booster club or other benefactor if such action would be in violation of NCAA rules. A violation of that term could result in the termination of Franchione's contract, which runs through 2012, per Section 5.1 (a) under Termination for Cause. Franchione can be suspended without pay or the agreement can be terminated immediately if he breaks any of the rules listed in Sections 2.1 through 2.5.

As is often the case with these NCAA rules violations, their discovery is pure luck, not the result of vigilant compliance officers who go over every receipt and phone log. For instance, Franchione was busted when his personal assistant was caught sending out the newsletter. Athletic Director Bill Byrne immediately fired the assistant, admonished Franchione, and ordered the coach to shut down his Web site.

After completing an internal investigation, Byrne said Franchione "did not intentionally, knowingly, or directly participate in actions that were inappropriate or in violation of rules or policies."

Maybe so, but Franchione took a buyout estimated to be worth more than $4 million over the next three years and stepped down less than an hour after Texas A&M upset rival Texas 38 to 30. Defensive coordinator Gary Darnell was named interim coach and led the Aggies through the rest of the season, including their December 29 Alamo Bowl game against Penn State.

Three days after Franchione resigned, Texas A&M announced that it had hired former Green Bay Packers coach Mike Sherman as their new head football coach. He had been an offensive line coach at Texas A&M under revered head football coach R. C. Slocum from 1989 through 1993 and in 1995–96. Sherman is paid $1.8 million a year.

The Aggies, who finished 7-5 overall and 4-4 in the Big 12 in 2007, ranked last in the Big 12 and 101st nationally in passing offense, averaging just 187 yards per game. Texas A&M had hoped that Sherman would improve that, but former NFL coaches have had spotty success at best in the college ranks. In 2008, the Aggies were 4-7. Similarly, former Oakland Raiders coach Bill Callahan was fired at the end of the 2007 season after four mediocre years at Nebraska. Former Dallas Cowboys coach Chan Gailey was fired after six seasons at Georgia Tech. Former Chicago Bears and Miami Dolphins Coach Dave Wannstedt has struggled at Pittsburgh. And, of course, the most well-documented (and some say, "cherished") meltdown of the past few college football seasons took place in South Bend, where after two strong seasons under former New England Patriots offensive coordinator Charlie Weis, Notre Dame set a school record for losses in 2007 with a record of 3-9. The 2008 season wasn't much better.

The one exception so far has been Pete Carroll, who guided New England to the AFC East title in 1997 and has led USC to two national championships since 2000.

"Stop me if you've heard this before," wrote ESPN college football writer Ivan Maisel. "A fallen Big 12 power believes the key to righting itself is by hiring a fired NFL head coach with a college background."

He went on to detail the former NFL coaches who have failed in college, but thinks Sherman is different.

"Sherman spent seven seasons coaching the Aggies' offensive line for R. C. Slocum," he wrote. "Sherman left behind a lot of believers in College Station, including Slocum, who has worked as a fundraiser since being fired after the 2002 season."

Even a lowly sport like college swimming is not immune to the temptation to cheat. In 2007, Stanford suspended men's swimming coach Skip Kenney for two months without pay for doctoring the team's record book. Athletic director Bob Bowlsby said no NCAA violations had been discovered and Kenney, who kept his job, apologized in a letter to the university community, "for my error in judgment. I had no right to omit the records of any athlete on media guides or other publications. This will not occur again."

This was no rookie mistake by a first-year coach. Kenney, sixty-four, has coached the team since 1979 and had led Stanford to seven NCAA titles and twenty-six straight Pac-10 championships.

In 2007, these scandals—and the rising salaries of college coaches—caught the eye of the House Ways and Means Committee. In October 2007, the committee asked the NCAA to justify why such a revenue-generating enterprise deserves tax-exempt status.

Chairman Bill Thomas, R-Calif., in a letter to NCAA president Myles Brand, said "excessive compensation . . . makes less revenue available for other sports, causes many athletic departments to operate at a net loss, and may call into question the priorities of educational institutions."

Thomas went on to ask, "What actions has the NCAA taken to encourage its member institutions to curb excessive compensation for college coaches?"

Brand has urged schools not to spend beyond their means, on facilities as well as on coaches. Ironically, the NCAA can't set financial parameters on individual schools without violating Congress's own antitrust laws.

Brand's answer to Congress, in part, was that much of the big money paid to coaches is underwritten by media, apparel, and other outside entities, and isn't coming out of university coffers.

Brand left out one important source of funding for coaches' salaries: boosters.

8 A BOOST UP

In April 2006, North Carolina State faced a bit of a financial dilemma. Men's basketball coach Herb Sendek left after ten mostly successful seasons. He traded his $800,000 a year job at N.C. State for a contract north of a million bucks to be the head basketball coach at Arizona State. Looking at the nationwide free market for top-notch college basketball coaches, N.C. State figured it would have to spend upward of $2 million to get the caliber of coach they wanted in Raleigh.

Some in North Carolina weren't sorry to see Sendek go. While he had an impressive .690 winning percentage, the more important record for North Carolina State fans was 17-54. That was his won-loss tally against Duke, North Carolina, and Wake Forest—N.C. State's fiercest rivals both locally and in the basketball-mad Atlantic Coast Conference. The Wolfpack faithful were tired of losing to these local teams, and they were willing to pay whatever it cost to change that losing record into a winning one. There was just one question: Where would they get the money?

Enter the Wolfpack Club. This group of wealthy N.C. State boosters was already paying N.C. State head football coach Chuck Amato an $840,000 annuity to keep him happy. (Before the annuity, he was already making $900,000 a year, including a base salary of $206,000 and a bonus of three months' pay whenever he takes N.C. State to a bowl game.) They were willing to do the same to land the right men's basketball coach.

As you learned in the last chapter, incentive packages paid to coaches by outside sources are not unique. The North Carolina Educational Foundation, the University of North Carolina booster group commonly known as the Ram's Club, raised $3.9 million for a "replacement package" to keep UNC men's basketball coach Roy Williams in Chapel Hill. And, of course, all of these payments are made through the school, thereby making them tax-exempt for both the school and the donor.

Welcome to the modern-day world of college sports boosters. It used to be that they were content just being enthusiastic fans. They tailgated before every home football game and made modest donations to the alumni association in exchange for courtside seats to home basketball games. Today, the donations have risen to the six-, seven-, and even the nine-figure range. That buys these mega-boosters access and privilege that would make most alumni blush. In addition to funding big-buck pay packages for top-tier coaches and building the $100 million stadiums and arenas in which their favorite college sports teams play, some boosters have considerable influence in deciding which coaches get hired and fired. That's certainly true of the Wolfpack Club.

In 2004, the latest year for which data are available, the Wolfpack Club raised $25.8 million. By comparison, the Iron Dukes, who passed the hat among distinguished Duke alumni, came up with just $18.2 million. UNC's Ram's Club raised a paltry $15.9 million. In addition to paying for scholarships (neither State nor UNC use public money for athletic scholarships), these booster groups also often help bankroll new facilities. In the past few years, N.C. State has used booster money to build new or updated venues for baseball, basketball, and football.

Of course, it helps that one of N.C. State's academic specialties is applied technology, and the school is in the middle of North Carolina's Research Triangle, home to some of America's most successful high-tech businesses. Two of North Carolina's four billionaires—Wendell Murphy and Jim Goodnight—are both North Carolina State alumni. The Wendell H. Murphy Football Center, a plush complex of offices, locker rooms, and training facilities, was built thanks to Mr. Murphy's generous $26 million check. Two of the founders of Cree Inc., a Durham, North Carolina, semiconductor manufacturer, are also N.C. State grads and dot-com multimillionaires.

THE MOST POWERFUL MAN IN NORTH CAROLINA

While having wealthy alumni certainly helps, it is Wolfpack Club executive director Bobby Purcell who makes the whole thing work. He was an assistant athletic director, mainly in charge of recruiting, before he took over the Wolfpack Club in 1997. According to many, he has the gift for gab that helps curry favor with—and money from—N.C. State's wealthiest alumni. He created the Student Wolfpack Club, to target future donors; the Junior Wolfpack Club for children; the Varsity Club for former athletes; and the Women of the Wolfpack. He personally returns phone calls from the nearly twenty thousand alumni—regardless of the size of their donation. Before most home football games he can be seen riding around the parking lots that surround Carter-Finley Stadium in a golf cart decked out in N.C. State colors, making sure everyone has the right parking pass and is having a good time. At kickoff, he's up in one of the luxury suites, schmoozing with the boosters that keep North Carolina State athletics flush with cash.

Purcell has overseen the construction of the RBC Center, where N.C. State plays basketball and the NHL's Carolina Hurricanes play their games. The facility, which seats 19,722 for basketball and 18,730 for hockey, cost $158 million and was funded primarily by an increase in the state's hotel and restaurant tax. The Hurricanes kicked in $20 million, too.

When N.C. State hired football coach Chuck Amato away from Florida State in 2000, Purcell fast-tracked the building of the Murphy Center. In addition to convincing Murphy to write the check, Purcell got him to loan the school his private jet so designers could fly around the country and look at other training facilities. Today, coaches and designers from around the country come to the Murphy Center to get ideas for their own facilities.

Purcell also oversaw the $97 million renovation of Carter-Finley Stadium. The multiphase project added fifty-one luxury suites and 1,000 club seats to the west grandstand, and 5,500 seats to the north end zone, bringing total capacity to 57,500. The alumni didn't have to contribute directly to the renovation, but they do purchase the lion's share of the suites, which rent for upward of $55,000 per season. The club seats cost $1,750 each per game.

So when N.C. State faced the prospect of having to pony up a cool two mil for a new basketball coach, it only made sense that they would turn to Purcell and the Wolfpack Club, who would have been only too happy to oblige.

"We have funds in place," Purcell said at the time.

Fortunately, they didn't need them. N.C. State ended up hiring Sydney Lowe, a point guard on Jim Valvano's 1983 championship-winning team. Lowe, a former assistant with the Detroit Pistons, earns about $900,000 a year. Under the terms of his contract, Lowe gets an annual income of $760,000, including $250,000 from Capitol Broadcasting for television and radio appearances. He also gets annual bonuses for making the NCAA tourney, endorsement money, and a $50,000 bonus every year the team's NCAA adjusted graduation rate is 55 percent or higher. Adidas had paid Sendek $80,000 a year as part of its apparel contract with N.C. State; Lowe reportedly has the same deal.

COWBOY UP

While it may sound like the Wolfpack Club, and its counterpart, the Ram's Club over at UNC, are spending a lot on athletics, they're in the low-rent district when it comes to today's alumni contributors. T. Boone Pickens, chairman of the billion-dollar energy hedge fund BP Capital Management, is an alumnus of Oklahoma State University. In early 2009, Pickens was number 131 on *Forbes* magazine's list of the richest Americans, with an estimated net worth of about $3 billion. He has given his alma mater some $300 million, with about 90 percent of it earmarked for athletics. In 2006 alone, he gave OSU $165 million, making it the single largest donation ever to a college athletic department. His name is on the School of Geology, his old fraternity house, and the lodge at Karsten Creek Golf Club. But it's most prominently displayed on the façade of Boone Pickens Stadium, where the Cowboys play their home football games each autumn.

Pickens also came up with what's perhaps the most bizarre—and brilliant—scheme in athletic fundraising history. Boosters designate OSU as the beneficiary of a $10 million life insurance policy. When they die, the money goes to the school. The program is called—are you ready for this?—"The Gift of a Lifetime."

All of Pickens's money not only buys naming rights, it buys access and privilege. And the right to complain about a football program that's only had modest success (OSU did beat Indiana in the 2008 Insight Bowl, 49 to 33, but lost to Oregon in the 2009 Pacific Life Holiday Bowl, 42 to 31).

"I don't know anything about football," he said in a 2006 ESPN interview. "I never criticize anything. I will say it didn't look like they were ready to play or something like that. That is as far as I go. They don't need somebody looking over their shoulder commenting. They know I am here."

"I do want to know what is going on," he said. "If we have a coaching change I want to be one of the first to know about it. If anybody is leaving or coming in, I sure want to be in on helping pick that person."

That's what $300 million will get you. But Pickens isn't the most prominent (or obnoxious) high-bucks booster. That distinction goes to Phil Knight, founder of Nike and alum of the University of Oregon. Like Pickens, most of Knight's postgraduate largesse has gone to the athletic department.

A KNIGHT IN SHINING ARMOR

Phil Knight actually began his boosterism by making donations to the academic side of the University of Oregon. In 1994, he gave $27.4 million to renovate what became the Knight Library. Two years later, he gave $10 million to build the William W. Knight Law Center, named after his dad, and another $15 million for endowed chairs and other law school faculty positions. It's just in the past decade or so that he's begun to lavish money on the Oregon athletic department.

Shortly after Oregon played in the 1995 Rose Bowl, Knight began a streak of athletic department donations that would eventually total about $70 million. Since then, he's funded half of the $90 million expansion of Autzen Stadium and contributed funds for the athletic department's $11 million home, the Casanova Center. Knight also paid for the majority of the $16 million Moshofsky Center, the Pacific Northwest's first indoor practice facility for football. The building is named after Ed Moshofsky, who played for Oregon in the 1940s and went on to be a successful lumberman. Moshofsky contributed just $2 million toward the project, but Knight insisted that the building be named for the former player, not its biggest benefactor.

In August 2007, Knight put himself in the same league as Pickens, announcing a $100 million donation to the athletic department to, in part, build a new indoor basketball arena. Thanks to Knight's donations over the years and the endowment he set up, Oregon is one of the handful of schools that claims its athletic department is self-funding. So what does a couple of hundred million dollars buy you in college sports today?

Knight is a frequent visitor to the Oregon locker room after games. He's been known to put on a headset to listen in on the plays coming down from the coaching booth. In his $90,000-per-season luxury suite, he writes out the keys to winning the game on a whiteboard and discusses them at length with guests, which often include the coaching staff. And, as one ESPN writer said in a 2006 profile, "Oregon folks coddle and fawn over their rich uncle at every turn." That includes the athletic department.

Knight and his wife, Penny, fly down to Oregon football games on their private jet. They're picked up at the airport by no less than Associate Athletic Director Jim Bartko, who then drives them to their private motor coach that is already parked in the lot outside the stadium. In addition to being Knight's chauffer, Bartko briefs him almost every day during the football season.

"Just to fill him in on what is happening," said Athletic Director Bill Moos. "And he is always excited about how recruiting is going."

Every offseason, head football coach Mike Bellotti and his two assistants actually go to Knight's home outside Portland and spend a few hours with him.

"He's a fan," Bellotti said, "but he is also enamored or excited about the intricacies of the game. He is a competitor. I think he looks at our strategies here and likes to say, 'How do you beat somebody with lesser personnel? Or similar personnel? Or better personnel? And what is the thought process going in?' He's excited to get the inner look."

In addition to his support for football and basketball, it's well known that Knight would like to see Oregon win a College World Series (Oregon State, much to his annoyance, has two CWS trophies in its display case). And he'd like to see the school's track and field program return to the glory days of Steve Prefontaine.

When Knight, a modestly successful middle distance runner, came to Oregon as a freshman in 1955, Eugene was known as "Track Town USA." He and his Oregon track coach, Bill Bowerman, went on to found Nike, and the program has never been the same.

Of course, having a rich benefactor such as Knight can cut both ways. It's widely understood that he orchestrated the firing of track coach Martin Smith, who Knight didn't think was doing a good enough job with his old program. And while Knight is also an alumnus of the Stanford Graduate School of Business, his $105 million donation to the school in 2006 was seen as a shot across the bow of Oregon, with the clear message that they'd better improve the track team, or else.

"He is undoubtedly the best-connected fan-booster in the United States, probably the world, because he lives so intensely in the world of competitive sports," Oregon president Dave Frohnmayer said fawningly. "And to have a person of that intellectual caliber, let alone of his loyalty to the University of Oregon, is striking, and it really shows."

"It is a relationship that has kept me here, because I know who he is," head football coach Bellotti admits. "And I trust him. He has never, ever asked me to do anything. He's never influenced anything. He lends his support, really his creative support. In fact, one time I had one of his [Nike] team managers come and talk to our coaches about sales, about how to sell something."

With Knight as a booster, Oregon has access not only to his bank account but to Nike's R&D department. When Nike introduced a new look in college uniforms in 1999, Oregon was the first to sport the new swag.

Pickens and Knight aren't alone in the nine-figure athletic booster club. And that has some people worried.

A TROUBLING TREND

According to the *Chronicle of Higher Education,* the country's biggest athletic departments—thanks in large part to their deep-pockets booster clubs and individual benefactors—raised more than $1.2 billion in 2006–7. Some programs have tripled their annual donations over the past decade. But all this athletic largesse has come at a cost, the *Chronicle* argues. While donations to the country's 119 largest athletics departments have risen significantly in recent years, overall giving to those colleges has stayed relatively flat. In 1998 athletic gifts accounted for 14.7 percent of all contributions. By 2003, the figure had risen to 26 percent and, many believe, continues to climb (Table 8.1).

In 2006, twenty-seven athletics programs raised more than $20 million each. Ten programs brought in more than $30 million. The University of North Carolina raised more than $51 million in 2006, the University of Virginia $45 million, and Ohio State $39 million.

Part of the reason for the increase in donations is thanks to operators like N.C. State's Bobby Purcell. Once content to host pregame tailgate parties and pass the can, athletic booster groups became increasingly more sophisticated—and aggressive—in their fundraising. Today they raise funds through multimillion-dollar licensing deals, affinity-credit-card programs, and, of course, preferred seating in luxury suites and stadium clubs. One booster club, Florida State's Seminole Boosters, is even going into hock to make sure its athletes (and boosters) have nothing but the best: it's secur-

TABLE 8.1

Big-Time College Sports Get Rising Share of Gifts

	Total gifts	Athletics gifts	Percentage of total gifts that went to athletics
1998	$5,841,124	$858,613	14.7%
1999	$6,337,790	$1,071,281	16.9%
2000	$7,330,109	$1,237,649	16.9%
2001	$8,683,508	$1,543,396	17.8%
2002	$7,327,726	$1,674,970	22.9%
2003	$8,095,027	$2,105,787	26.0%

Source: Jeffrey L. Stinson and Dennis R. Howard, in Brad Wolverton, "Growth in Sports Gifts May Mean Fewer Academic Donations," *Chronicle of Higher Education,* Oct. 5, 2007.
Note: The figures cover gifts by alumni to the 119 NCAA Division I-A institutions and show average gifts.

ing (and guaranteeing) $70 million of debt to pay for improvements to the university's athletics facilities.

Donations to athletics, including personal seat licenses, which start at $2,000 and go into the six figures at places like Kentucky, have led some donors to cut back their contributions to other parts of the college, says Jeffrey L. Stinson, an assistant professor of marketing at North Dakota State University, who has studied the effect of athletics fundraising on total giving to colleges.

"We don't necessarily see a decrease on a dollar-for-dollar basis," he said. "But you do see donors cut back a little on that academic gift because they just don't have the capacity."

Some booster clubs are taking a page from the credit card companies' playbook and allowing non-athletic contributions to count toward points that earn boosters privileges. It's much like your airline credit card, which racks up frequent flier miles even when you're paying for groceries or gas. The booster clubs allow donations to academic departments to count toward earning perks as an athletic booster. So a donation to the English department can help get a booster enough points to earn courtside seats for home basketball games.

And although big-name (and big-bucks) boosters such as Pickens and Knight get most of the publicity, many booster clubs are seeing the greatest increases in athletic funding from small donors. For instance, LSU's booster club brought in $35 million in 2006. Its biggest gains came from boosters who gave just $100,000. And the number of LSU boosters who gave just $5,000 doubled to more than two hundred. That may not sound like much compared with Pickens and Knight, but securing alumni donations is a long-term game. Booster clubs are hoping that the young alumnus giving $5,000 today will give more as his or her personal fortune increases.

"With that amount of money, you get a guy who's on his way up," said Ron Richard, chief executive officer of the LSU boosters. "He's not a millionaire yet, but he's going to be."

And though Phil Knight is surely the only Oregon booster who gets daily updates from the athletic director's office and a personal briefing by coaches, other boosters are getting pretty decent perks.

Wake Forest, which has just 4,400 members in its alumni association, recently created the Moricle Society for donors who contribute at least $55,000 a year. The program has brought in an extra $1 million a year for the athletic department. In exchange, members fly free to away games on the team's charter flights and get private "chalk talks" from coaches before games.

"We don't skimp on these people," said Cook Griffin, executive director of Wake Forest's Deacon Club. "You can't spend too much on them."

Sometimes, high-profile coaches are brought in as the closer on deals that benefit academic departments. University of Louisville basketball coach Rick Pitino was brought in to visit a prospective donor and close the deal for a big donation to Louisville's medical school. At LSU, the booster club and LSU Foundation, the university's general fundraising arm, work together. Over the years, the booster club has helped arrange $8 million in donations to academic programs.

This is a marked change from twenty years ago, when athletics ran a distant second to academics in terms of fundraising.

"They were the guys doing the golf tournaments, and no one took them seriously," said fundraising consultant Bruce Flessner. "Now they've pushed themselves front and center, and they're eating a big slice of the philanthropic pie."

MORE THAN CHEERLEADERS

Of course, sometimes boosters do more than cheer. They break the rules, by giving athletes no-show jobs (before, during, and after their NCAA eligibility), slipping them some cash, or buying them the new suit or tricked-out Tahoe they can't afford on their $100 a month scholarship allowance.

The NCAA's Infractions Committee ruled that Arkansas had committed three major violations and one secondary infraction of the rules governing payments to student-athletes. The NCAA found that from 1994 through 1999, at least twenty football and basketball players were overpaid an estimated $4,300 for part-time jobs at J&H Truck Service in Dallas. The business is owned by university booster Ted Harrod, who gave more than $285,000 to Arkansas athletic programs from 1987 through 2000. During its investigation, the NCAA found that the athletic department wasn't vigilant enough in monitoring the jobs and that the overpayments were intentional.

"I don't think there's any belief that it was inadvertent," Infractions Committee chairman Tom Yeager said in a press release.

Harrod argued that it was. He said he was set up by his former daughter-in-law, who was angry at Harrod and trying to get back at him. The NCAA interviewed her and dismissed much of her testimony, but still found that Harrod had intentionally tried to circumvent NCAA rules.

Arkansas paid about $250,000 to an outside consulting firm to conduct its own investigation, and thousands more defending itself against the charges. In the end, the school increased oversight of high-dollar boosters and athletes' jobs, and added a second full-time employee for compliance issues.

"Integrity is on my mind and our staff's mind every day," Arkansas athletic director Frank Broyles said during a press conference. "That's been my priority ever since I became a coach. We're working just as hard to eliminate unintentional mistakes and mistakes by people outside the athletic department."

Starting with the 2006 school year, Arkansas was allowed to award the maximum eighty-five football scholarships for the first time since the 2000–2001 school year. During the probationary period, the school lost ten football scholarships and one men's basketball scholarship. Arkansas spent about $250,000 in private funds on an outside consultant and thousands more investigating and defending itself. The school made several changes to improve its NCAA rules compliance system. It stepped up oversight of high-access boosters and athletes' jobs, and it increased NCAA compliance education for its coaches, staff, athletes, and boosters. Arkansas also added a second full-time employee for compliance issues. Although the school is off probation, it is on what the NCAA calls "repeat violator status." If another major infraction occurs within five years, the penalties will be much harsher.

That's all well and good, but looking at it purely in economic terms, how harsh was Arkansas's penalty for violating NCAA rules?

Arkansas lost eleven scholarships (ten football and one basketball). In-state tuition is about $9,000 a year. Add in room and board and we'll round it off to $15,000. Out of state, it's roughly double that. So at most, the violation cost the university (which is reimbursed by the athletic department for scholarships) $330,000; at least, about $165,000. Let's high-ball the cost of the investigation and say they spent another $500,000. If we round everything up, the total cost to Arkansas of the NCAA rules violations was about $1 million.

Arkansas has a $44 million athletic budget. On January 1, 2008, two years after coming off probation, Arkansas played Missouri in the AT&T Cotton Bowl, which paid each team $2.8 million. In other words, in just one bowl game appearance, Arkansas made nearly three times what it paid for committing the NCAA infractions. In today's high-dollar world of college athletics, is $1 million really a deterrent? Hardly.

Of course, no matter how economically ineffective the NCAA penalties are, some boosters have had better success in defending themselves against allegations of wrongdoing. *The* high-profile booster case of the 2007–8 season was that of Ray Keller, the Alabama booster who sued the NCAA for defamation—and won.

In December 2007, a Jackson County, Alabama, jury awarded Keller $5 million. The lawsuit against the NCAA stemmed from a February 2002 NCAA Infractions Report that found recruiting violations at Alabama and placed the school on five years' probation. The report referred to Keller and two other boosters as "parasites," "pariahs," and "rogue boosters." The boosters were not named in the report, but were later identified in media reports. Keller claimed he was innocent of violating NCAA rules and said the report not only tarnished his reputation but cost him at least one lucrative business deal.

Radio sports talk show host Paul Finebaum took the witness stand in the case and said that "he had never heard such language used about boosters," the Associated Press reported. He also said the NCAA's 2002 press conference to announce sanctions against the Alabama football program was "extremely negative." Finebaum said of the NCAA, "I think it's an organization that uses its power to destroy the people they select."

During the trial, the NCAA said Keller repeatedly broke—or at least stretched—its rules in regard to his relationship with current student-athletes and prospective recruits.

"He refused to obey warnings from both (former Alabama athletics director) Hootie Ingram and (current athletics director) Mal Moore," one of the NCAA's attorneys said. "He knew the rules but did it anyway. That is the character at issue."

Boosters certainly know the rules—or should. Here are excerpts from a reminder posted by the University of Texas Athletic Department:

Dear Alumni, UT Faculty and Staff, and Friends:

Two of the important cornerstones of University of Texas Athletics are the loyalty and enthusiasm of Longhorn fans who have demonstrated by their interest in our teams and their attendance at events that they are without equal.

The UT athletics departments appreciate this marvelous fan support, which stimulates and encourages our student-athletes and energizes our entire organization. We must be cautious, however, not to let enthusiasm for athletics lead us into conflict with the very specific rules and regulations of the National Collegiate Athletic Association or the Big 12 Conference.

The NCAA definition of "a representative of the University's athletics interests" is very broad and encompasses many—if not all—of the people who are regular attendees at our sports events. If you fall into this category, there are a number of activities regarding contact with student-athletes and recruits that could put the University at risk for NCAA sanctions.

We have summarized the applicable NCAA rules in this pamphlet. Please take the time to read it carefully, and should you have any questions, call the athletics compliance office at (512) 471-7285.

The University is charged with the responsibility to exercise "institutional control" of its athletics programs. We are committed to maintaining responsible programs.

The University of Texas is grateful for all you have done to make this one of the nation's model programs. We know, based on our contacts with the alumni, UT faculty and staff, and friends across the state and the country, that you share our earnest ambition for athletics success achieved within the rules.

Gratefully,
DeLoss Dodds—Director of Men's Athletics
Chris Plonsky—Director of Women's Athletics

Of course, boosters such as Harrod and Keller are typically the exception, not the rule. But with every scandal comes the klieg lights of the media, so these few rule-breaking boosters give the appearance of being the norm. In fact, the average booster is more like sixty-eight-year-old Dan Bird, a 1962 graduate of Kansas State's School of Animal Husbandry. Bird, who lives in tiny Anthony, Kansas, population 2,400, has built his small business into one of the largest commercial cattle feedlots in the country. As he has prospered, so has K-State.

Bird and his wife, Beth, a 1961 K-State graduate, have given more than $750,000 to their alma mater over the past four decades. Their donations were used to build the new $12 million alumni center, as well as the new Jack Veneer athletic complex that features a new state-of-the-art training room and coaches' offices.

"It's the most money I've given to anything in my life," Bird says of his K-State donations. In addition to athletics, Bird's financial gifts helped build the arch outside the university's new art museum and have helped fund scholarships for agricultural economics. He even sat on the library board.

"I used it only in my freshman and senior year," he said with a chuckle, "so I figured I needed to spend some more time there."

Where the Birds spend most of their time is at K-State football and basketball games. They've long had season tickets for football, and with the arrival of coach Bob Huggins bought tickets for men's basketball, as well. They go to almost every home and away football game, and attended the 1992 Tokyo Bowl. More important, they've never bought a dinner for a player, slipped a player illegal cash, or tried to pay off a teacher to give a player a better grade.

"I've never seen anything like that," said Bird. "And frankly, I can't imagine it happening at K-State."

He's not alone. While it's a popular misconception that boosters are a gang of corrupt thugs who would do anything and everything to see their team win, nothing could be further from the truth. Most are just your average fans, happy to cheer on their team and give what they can, usually just four or five-figure donations, to their alma mater.

The myth of the corrupt booster, of course, is perpetuated by a media culture that magnifies every transgression. And they'd never think of doing a feature on the Dan Birds of the booster world. As a result, the bad boosters appear to be the norm.

Robert L. Simon, a professor of philosophy at Hamilton College in upstate New York, defended the integrity of intercollegiate athletics at the NCAA's Scholarly Colloquium on College Sports in Nashville in January 2008.

"Some critics will argue for the moral bankruptcy of intercollegiate athletics, citing such examples as academic fraud in one major basketball program, falsification of academic records in order to insure eligibility for an athlete at another, misbehavior including alleged criminal acts by some recruited athletes, and dismal graduation rates in some high-visibility men's programs," Dr. Simon said in his keynote address. "However, it is important to remember that intercollegiate sports occur at a wide variety of institutions, ranging over different divisions and different educational missions. The problems of some high-profile Division I programs, particularly in men's high-visibility sports, are not always typical of the wide variety of intercollegiate programs found across the nation."

Simon is absolutely correct. The vast majority of student-athletes go through college without breaking the rules, receiving favorable treatment in the classroom, or being paid under the table. That's because for every high-profile football and basketball player, there are a hundred other athletes in non-revenue sports such as soccer, swimming, track and field, and crew. These sports haven't been corrupted by the media-driven financial frenzy of college football and basketball. But perception is reality. None other than Andrew Zimbalist, the noted sports economist, buys into the media-driven myth that all athletes are somehow on the take.

"Like the airlines which, unable to compete over prices prior to deregulation, lavished resources on travel amenities and advertising, college coaches, unable to compete over top high school prospects with salary offers, lavish millions of dollars on recruitment and special services for athletes once in college," Zimbalist said. "Then they arrange for 'boosters' (usually sports-crazed local businessmen) to make payments on the side to their athletes, while salivating sports agents and their lackeys dangle dollars before the immature, impecunious athletes attempting to induce them to sign over 5 percent of their future earnings should they become pros."

While I respect Zimbalist, this is a misperception, even if it comes from one of the most respected sports economists in the business. But I can excuse this misperception because, as I'll show in the next chapter, the number of athletes and coaches who fit the stereotype was on full display in 2007, making it one of the most profligate years of cheating and scandals in college sports history.

9 BREAKIN' ALL THE RULES

In the foreword to his 2005 memoir, *Runnin' Rebel,* former UNLV coach Jerry Tarkanian wrote, "In major college basketball, nine out of 10 teams break the rules. The other one is in last place."

How right he is. I have to say, this was the hardest chapter of the book to write. When I started, my research had yielded 45,000 words. And I'd been fairly judicious in my research. I only chose the "big scandals" at the "big schools." I easily could have written a 100,000-word book just on NCAA violations.

MIDWEST MADNESS

In 2007–8, the NCAA was headed toward a record year in terms of team violations and probations. And to the casual fan, it must have looked like there was something in the water in the Midwest. At a glance, it appeared as if all the big programs in the region were on probation. But as with everything else in today's confusing world of college athletics, all was not as it seemed.

The biggest—and most legitimate—scandal of the 2007–8 season involved Indiana University basketball coach Kelvin Sampson. The coach, who had only been around college athletics for twenty-eight years, participated in ten three-way telephone calls with prospective recruits. That's not unusual. A lot of times, the assistant coach in charge of recruiting will be on the road, have a kid and his parents on the phone, and conference in the head coach. There was just one problem. Sampson wasn't supposed to be on *any* telephone calls with recruits because he was already on NCAA probation. Just seventeen months earlier, while he was the coach at Oklahoma, the NCAA had found that Sampson had participated in "excessive" phone calls to recruits—577 excessive phone calls, to be exact. The NCAA banned Sampson from off-campus recruiting for one year and barred him from initiating phone contact with prospects. Even though the allegations were hanging over his head, Indiana hired Sampson to replace Mike Davis, who had previously been hired for the unenviable job of succeeding legendary Indiana basketball coach Bob Knight. Although Indiana didn't fire Sampson for the recruiting violations that occurred while he was in Bloomington, it did dock him $500,000 of his $1.6 million salary. The school also lost one basketball scholarship for one year.

In an editorial, the *Terre Haute Tribune Star* said, "IU took its knocks for Knight's eccentricities and for Davis' meltdowns under immense pressure. But one charge Hoosier basketball hasn't had to own is cheating. This circumstance is even more troubling because Sampson should have taken extreme measures to avoid a repeat offense, particularly if he understood the institutional value of the IU program's clean NCAA track record. If the NCAA infractions committee concludes that Sampson deliberately skirted the rules, IU should replace him, reprimand [athletic director Rick] Greenspan and leave no doubt that such actions will not be explained away. Maybe the term 'zero tolerance' is appropriate."

How did Indiana discover these recruiting violations? The way most programs discover most NCAA rules violations: by pure luck. An intern noticed the three-way calls while compiling an NCAA-mandated report on recruiting practices.

"The intern was double-checking phone records in our compliance department and noticed the three-way call," Larry MacIntyre, Indiana's vice president of university communications told the Associated Press.

The university immediately began an investigation by attorney Robin Green Harris. She works for Ice Miller in Indianapolis, one of a handful of law firms that make a small fortune investigating allegations of inappropriate conduct by college athletic programs. In fact, they not only conduct the investigation but also recommend the punishment. And here's the kicker: nine times out of ten the NCAA says, "OK" to the investigation, findings, and recommended punishment.

Why, you may ask, does the school conduct the investigation and why are all schools expected to police themselves and report such violations? Because the NCAA, which brings in hundreds of millions of dollars a year in revenue to oversee what is supposed to be amateur athletics, and has enough money to pay President Myles Brand about $1 million a year, has just a handful of compliance investigators, most of them young kids fresh out of graduate school.

"It was a broad and collaborative process in determination of the sanctions," A. D. Greenspan told the *Indianapolis Star*.

Surprisingly, the greatest outrage to Sampson's repeat recruiting violation came not from the Indiana administration but from former players. Two-time All-American Kent Benson called the situation "a total travesty" and said he was "totally embarrassed for the Indiana basketball program."

"They need to do the right thing," Benson told the *Indianapolis Star*. "If no tolerance means no tolerance, then get rid of him. And Greenspan should be right behind."

Former player Ted Kitchel was less kind in his comments to the newspaper. When Sampson was hired, he said, "I wouldn't hire that guy to coach my fifth-grade girls team." When he learned of the recruiting violations, he said that Sampson obviously didn't think the rules applied to him.

So what are the economic lessons we can take away from the Kelvin Sampson case? He was making $1 million a year at Oklahoma and was caught making 577 illegal recruiting phone calls. While he was still under investigation, Indiana hired him. He was supposed to make $1.6 million in 2007–8. Instead, he made just $1.1 million. In January 2008, Indiana was ranked in the Top 25 and still had standout basketball recruit Eric Gordon.

"Is Eric Gordon and a national championship worth $500,000?'" an Indiana alumnus asked in the *Indianapolis Star*. "I say, yes."

I'd agree. And while I think it's fair to say that Sampson knew what he was doing when he broke the rules, it's also easy to understand when a coach or athletic director or even a school's compliance officer stumbles over the four-hundred-page NCAA rulebook and makes an honest mistake. Very few have read it all the way through, and fewer claim to understand all of its intricacies.

TOO MANY RULES, NOT ENOUGH REFEREES

One problem with the NCAA rulebook is that it is so broad. It covers kids from high school through college and into the pros. It covers not only their behavior on the court but also the behavior of their parents, their aunts, their uncles, their high school and college coaches, and hundreds of thousands of boosters. If any one of these people violates the rulebook, it is the university, not the individual, that is penalized. And even if the university had an army of investigators and compliance officers overseeing their athletes, it would be impossible to watch them every minute of every day.

A Penn State alum and avid booster I know tells a funny story about Shane Conlin, the All-American linebacker who played for Coach Joe Paterno in the mid-1980s and was picked in the first round of the NFL Draft by the Buffalo Bills. In the spring of his senior year, after his NCAA eligibility had expired, Conlin played in a charity golf tournament sponsored by the Elks Club. After they were done playing golf, they went into the clubhouse and one of the guys in Conlin's foursome went to the bar to buy a round of drinks. Conlin almost tackled the guy as he walked toward the bar. Even though his eligibility had expired, Penn State had obviously trained Conlin to be on the lookout for any potentially embarrassing recruiting violations. As a result, Conlin wouldn't even let a booster buy him a Coke after a round of golf, fearing that someone would see it and report it.

That's an interesting and humorous story, but it also is the reality for every Division I program in the country. I doubt anyone would have made a big deal of a booster buying Shane Conlin a Coke. Furthermore, I doubt anyone would have ever found out about it. But the point is that Penn State would have been held accountable—and quite possibly put on probation—had Conlin received the gift of a fifty-cent Coke. More important, how many times does a scene like this happen in any given school year? How can Penn State—or any school—possibly be expected to police the Elks Club in Boalsburg, Pennsylvania, and know whether or not boosters—or even casual fans—are buying a soda for a Penn State football player? This is the world—and nightmare—that every athletic director faces. And while there are certainly serious recruiting and academic violations occurring on campuses across the country every day, some of these missteps are the result of an overly broad NCAA rulebook that is sometimes confusing and contradictory.

Take Kelvin Sampson's 577 illegal phone calls when he was at Oklahoma. It was a clear violation of NCAA rules. But before the NCAA passed a rule in 2007 barring coaches from text messaging players, Sampson could have text messaged those recruits 57,777 times and been in full compliance with the NCAA rulebook.

Coaches seemed split on the text messaging ban in 2007. Some were against the text messaging ban, saying text messaging was a good way to keep in touch with players. Others hated it.

"It puts a lot of pressure not only on your recruiting staff, but on the head coach," said Kansas State basketball coach Frank Martin.

"If Kansas texts a kid seven times a day, that means I have to text him at least eight times a day to show him I really want him," said Martin. "Where does it end?"

Where it ended for one prospect was in a sky-high cell phone bill. Patrick Patterson, the highly recruited power forward from Huntington, West Virginia, was being wooed by Duke, Florida, Kentucky, Virginia, and Wake Forest. In the month before he signed with Kentucky, he received more than seven thousand text messages, resulting in a $500 cell phone bill.

ALL IN THE FAMILY

Here's another NCAA rulebook contradiction. According to NCAA rules, coaches aren't supposed to find jobs with boosters for family members of recruits, but it's OK to hire them to work for the basketball program. In 2005, Ronnie Chalmers, father of standout point guard Mario Chalmers, was hired by the Kansas basketball team. He told the *Kansas City Star*, "Mario's decision to choose Kansas was solely based on Mario. [My wife] Almarie and I made a decision to stay in Alaska until she retired this spring, then relocate to follow Mario. This is a great opportunity to get my foot in the door at the college level, follow my son and be a part of one of the best programs in the country."

If Kansas had arranged for Ronnie Chalmers to work at a local car dealership owned by a booster, it would have been a clear violation of NCAA rules. But because they hired him in-house, although he had no college coaching experience (he'd been a high school coach in Anchorage), it was kosher with the NCAA.

Similarly, schools are prohibited from paying or providing any sort of gifts to a recruit's high school coach, but they can hire him for their sports camps. In 2006, the *Dallas Morning News* looked at the summer hiring practices of Big 12 teams and found that many paid speaking fees to the high school coaches of prominent recruits. For instance, Kansas paid three coaches associated with Darrell Arthur, a standout recruit from South Oak Cliff high school in Texas.

"Arthur's high school coach and two coaches associated with his summer play for years were all paid $2,000 to speak at the basketball camps held at Kansas the previous summer," the paper said. "They were among seven high school and summer league coaches to earn $2,000 as speakers at Kansas during one camp session that summer. None of the other 175 camp employees that year earned more than $600 per session. And all seven had something in common. They had coached current or former Jayhawks or had coached a high school player who signed with Kansas in 2005–6."

"This does not break the letter of the law, but I certainly do believe it violates the spirit of the law," said John Gerdy, a visiting professor of sports administration at Ohio University who has written a number of books on sports ethics.

The paper also found that the top-paid high school coach at the University of Texas's summer camp was an assistant coach at Nacogdoches High School who was paid $3,200. Nacogdoches was the alma mater of Damion James, who signed with Texas in May. Three members of the coaching staff at Seagoville High School earned $3,000 working camps for Texas A&M. Seagoville head coach Robert Allen was paid $1,800 for three sessions. Seagoville seniors Derrick Roland and Donald Sloan both had signed with the Aggies.

College coaches are also barred from watching voluntary offseason workouts. But they are allowed to have offices that overlook practice facilities where offseason workouts take place. As with the fifty-cent Coke at the

Boalsburg Elks Club, who's watching to make sure that the coach doesn't peek out his window and check out the players? The short answer is: nobody. This was the case in August 2009, when allegations surfaced that University of Michigan athletes were conducting offseason practices beyond NCAA guidelines.

The NCAA rule that seems most open to blatant violation is the one regarding official and unofficial campus visits. If a college basketball coach invites a recruit to campus, it's considered an official visit. Players are only allowed so many official visits per year per school (they vary by time of year and sport). All the coach has to do is fill out a form that says, "O. J. Mayo came to campus today for an official visit." They put it in their file in case the NCAA or one of the investigating law firms comes asking questions.

But a player can come on campus and watch practice any time he or she wants. Furthermore, coaches can leave tickets for players at the will call window for home basketball games and it doesn't count as an official visit. Again, unless the NCAA or the university has investigators watching every college practice in the country, how do they know if a kid's there for an official or an unofficial visit?

"A lot of local kids came to our practices in Cincinnati four or five days a week," said Frank Martin. "As long as they came, and we didn't invite them, it was considered an unofficial visit."

As ridiculous as this all sounds, the NCAA actually follows up on some of this stuff. In December 2006, Ohio State was forced to investigate a spaghetti-dinner fundraiser held in Akron to raise money for the parents of starting tailback Antonio Pittman; his backup, Chris Wells; defensive end Lawrence Wilson; and defensive back DeAngelo Haslam. Ohio State was headed to Glendale, Arizona, on January 8, 2007, to play in the BCS Championship game (they lost to Florida, 41 to 14). The fundraiser was held to raise money so that the players' parents could afford to make the trip.

"The bottom line on this issue is, Did these student-athletes receive an extra benefit or not?" said NCAA spokesman Bob Williams in a press release. "Everything that I have heard is that they did not."

Ohio State sports information director Steve Snapp said the investigation found no violations.

"It does clear us with the NCAA because if we don't self-report anything, there's nothing to investigate," he told the Associated Press. "This is clearly a non-violation. No eligibilities will be affected at all. It's a non-issue."

"We have thoroughly investigated this situation and feel confident that no rule violations occurred," Doug Archie, Ohio State's associate director of athletics for compliance, said in a written statement. "We have talked to all the principals involved and are confident that the players and their families had no prior knowledge of the event. Additionally, no money was given to anyone associated with the Ohio State football program. Those are the litmus tests."

MEANWHILE, BACK IN INDIANA

While Indiana was dealing with the fallout from the Kelvin Sampson recruiting scandal, over at Ball State in Muncie, Indiana, Ronnie Thompson resigned in July 2007 after just one season as the men's basketball coach. The son of legendary Georgetown basketball coach John Thompson, he led the Cardinals to a 9-22 record in 2006. He and his staff had been accused of attending voluntary offseason workouts, which, as stated earlier, is a violation of NCAA rules. They were also accused of lying about it when confronted by Ball State administrators.

In late 2007, Thompson was cleared of any wrongdoing. Furthermore, it was learned that part of the reason that he left the university was that Thompson, who is black, felt that he was being discriminated against on the predominantly white campus. An outside review was conducted by former Indiana Supreme Court Justice Myra Selby, who is also black, and she found no basis for allegations that the university had unlawfully discriminated against Thompson. Ball State submitted a report to the NCAA saying there was no evidence Thompson violated any NCAA ethical rules.

Selby did report that notes including racial slurs and insults had been slipped under the office doors of Thompson and his basketball staff in June 2007. Selby's investigation found "evidence of isolated incidents of racially hostile or insensitive behaviors on the part of a few athletic department employees," but they were not enough to create "an unlawful racially hostile environment." Ball State apologized to Thompson in a written statement to the university community, alumni, and boosters and fired the athletic department staffer who sent the notes.

"With respect to Coach Thompson, Ball State wishes to extend its sincere apology for the unprofessional and unauthorized behavior of its employees that led to his resignation, for the unfortunate distress that resulted from these actions, and for the unwarranted negative effect on his reputation."

It took six months to investigate the allegations. Why so long? Because like the NCAA, most schools have skeleton staffs in their athletic and academic compliance departments. In other words, the message seems to be that if there's any wrongdoing going on, most would rather not know about it.

The Mid-American Conference, or MAC, in which Ball State plays its games, is a good example of compliance staffing. Ball State has nineteen varsity sports and more than four hundred athletes, and in 2005–6 spent $1.1 million just on travel. It has one compliance officer. Its last major infraction was October 16, 2007. The school was found to be giving excessive financial aid, excessive grants-in aid, and impermissible extra benefits; had exceeded practice limitation; and was found to have a lack of institutional control. The sports involved included football, softball, and men's tennis. For these misdeeds, the school and coaches were given a public reprimand and censure, and two years' probation; the softball team was limited to a maximum of eighteen hours per week of practice; the school lost three football scholarships for two years; and the men's tennis team's financial aid was reduced by .04 of one grant.

Miami University is in the same situation as Ball State. It, too, has nineteen varsity sports, more than four hundred athletes, and only one compliance officer. Its last major infraction was January 17, 1991, when it was learned that the men's basketball coach had fraudulently given a player an A in a class to maintain his NCAA academic eligibility. In addition to a public reprimand and two years' probation, any individual and team records were stricken from the books, and the school forfeited all games in which the ineligible student participated.

Eight of the eleven core MAC schools have at least a director overseeing compliance issues and at least one full-time assistant. Buffalo and Northern

Illinois employ three full-time staffers, as well as graduate assistants and interns. Ball State is a one-man shop, with the exception of a graduate assistant who works five to ten hours a week.

"If it was up to me, I'd have more people," said Kyle Brennan, the director of athletics compliance and eligibility at Ball State. "It's really just me. That is low for the MAC. I'm grateful to athletic director Tom Collins and president Jo Ann Gora for the GA. I've tried to get more people on the staff to keep up with every team and all the NCAA requirements."

Looking at the four-hundred-page NCAA manual that sits on his desk, Brennan said, "It's not a pop-up book. It seems to be written by lawyers for lawyers. They read just like statutes."

Maybe so, but you don't have to be a lawyer to recognize some of the violations. For instance, a few years ago Ball State found that eighty-nine athletes in ten sports had received textbooks they didn't need, paid for with scholarship money. Instead of returning them, they gave the books to friends. That was before Brennan, a former probation litigation attorney from Denver, became the compliance officer. When asked about the size of the compliance staff, Ball State University president Gora said, "I don't think any of the violations would have been avoided with more people. I don't think the number of compliance officers is key, but what they do and how they function."

Maybe so, but Brennan's entire budget—including his salary—is less than $100,000. By comparison, Melody Reifel Werner, Eastern Michigan's compliance director, has a budget twice that size.

With compliance staffs this small, it's a wonder so many violations are discovered. Either schools are particularly vigilant in policing themselves, or the violations that are reported are only the tip of the iceberg. Here's a short list of some other recent NCAA violations:

In spring 2007, Clemson reported that an athlete's brother got free transportation, lodging, and meals from a booster while attending one of the school's road games.

In May 2007, Temple was placed on two years' probation when it reported that its men's tennis coach, Bill Hoehne, had told an ineligible athlete to play under someone else's name. According to the school, the coach hid the student's true identity by mumbling his name during prematch introductions. The school had to forfeit all matches from the 2004–5 academic year in which the student participated. The team was 3-9 that season.

Alabama football reported that a booster had "impermissible contact" with a recruit in a skybox at Bryant-Denny Stadium, a member of the coaching staff "provided improper transportation for a recruit's mother," and a booster gave a recruit a book.

South Carolina reported that it improperly used the photo of a current athlete in a summer football camp brochure.

Perhaps the biggest penalty of 2007 was levied against Oklahoma. The NCAA ruled that the Sooners must erase their wins from the 2005 season and lose two scholarships for the 2008–9 and 2009–10 school years. The penalties stemmed from a case involving two players, including starting quarterback Rhett Bomer, who were kicked off the team for being paid for work they had not performed at a Norman, Oklahoma, car dealership. The NCAA found Oklahoma guilty of a "failure to monitor" the employment of the players.

Of course, the case that everyone continues to monitor is the investigation into Reggie Bush and what he did—if anything—with a sports marketer while still at USC.

In January 2008, sports marketing agent Ben Delanoy claimed he spoke with Bush about developing a Web site before the Southern California tailback played his final game for the Trojans and won the Heisman Trophy.

"I said: 'Listen, you're one of the biggest names out there. You could be making a lot of money through this thing. We'll get your jersey on sale there and autographed items, pretty much soup to nuts.'" Delanoy told Yahoo! Sports that David Caravantes of New Era Sports and Entertainment took part in the three-way call. Caravantes denied the conversation took place and said he had spoken with Bush only once.

"Whatever that guy (Delanoy) is saying is absolutely false," Caravantes told Yahoo!.

Bush was also under pressure from a book, *Tarnished Heisman,* that claimed to have transcripts of conversations between New Era founder Lloyd Lake, Bush, and Bush's stepfather, Lamar Griffin. In some of the transcripts, Lake and Griffin discuss money and payment. New Era, which has since gone out of business, was founded in November 2005 and planned to make Bush its major client. Lake and his partner Michael Michaels have said they provided Bush and his family with nearly $300,000 in cash and other benefits while he was still playing at USC. The NCAA and Pac-10 were investigating whether Bush and his parents took improper payments while he was still at USC. Bush, who could lose his Heisman if the NCAA determines that he violated rules, has denied any wrongdoing.

Whether he's guilty or not, cheating in college athletics doesn't always have the most dire consequences. Just ask Rhett Bomer, the quarterback at the heart of the Oklahoma payola scandal. On August 31, 2008 the *Houston Chronicle* ran the headline, "OU transfer hits 16-of-24 in victory over Angelo State."

"Rhett Bomar still wears No. 7," the paper said. That's about the only thing that has not changed during his one-year exile from football. When he ran onto the field for Sam Houston State's season opener against Division II Angelo State, there was no deafening roar from the bleachers. The game wasn't on television. It wasn't a sellout. A crowd of 10,517 showed up at Bowers Stadium on Thursday night—one of the largest home openers in years for the Bearkats—but that's still a fraction of what Bomar played in front of on Saturdays to begin his college career at Oklahoma.

This isn't Norman anymore. For Bomar, that's just fine.

"I've moved on completely," Bomar told the paper. "I don't let anybody talk to me about the past. Now that I've got this first game under my belt, people can talk about Sam Houston."

In other words, all is forgotten, all is forgiven. And that includes the NCAA.

10 THE NCAA: CARTEL OR MAFIA?

In 2010, any serious observers of the big business of college athletics should be asking themselves one question: What's the difference between the NCAA president and fictional mob boss Tony Soprano?

If you talked to the residents of Tony Soprano's leafy neighborhood in suburban New Jersey, they'd tell you that he runs a number of successful and legitimate businesses. But as viewers of the hit HBO series *The Sopranos* know, he's a mob boss. His so-called legitimate businesses are merely a façade. Their primary purpose is to mask the real business that's going on behind the scenes: extortion, loan sharking, gambling, prostitution, and, sometimes, murder for hire. Tony Soprano is largely engaged in a criminal enterprise, and all his associates know it. So how does he keep them in line? The same way he keeps his customers in line: fear and intimidation.

Despite the fact that the majority of Tony Soprano's businesses are criminal enterprises, there are rules. Don't lie. Don't steal. Don't cheat. And don't get caught. If his underlings break these rules, the penalties are harsh. They might get a beating, lose part of their territory, have to give up some of their revenue, or, in some cases, get whacked. The NCAA operates much the same way.

THE FRONT OF AMATEURISM

The NCAA's front business is amateurism. The whole operation—the rules and regulations, the investigations, the seminars on balancing academics and athletics, and the ludicrous term *student-athlete*—are designed to hide the real business that the NCAA and their participating schools are engaged in: extortion. Viewed in the harshest—I would say "candid"—terms, they are extorting money from the (mostly poor and mostly black) kids who provide the raw material for the sports-entertainment business that generates billions of dollars for the NCAA and participating schools every year.

Think about it. The way the NCAA shakes down a student-athlete is no different from the way Tony Soprano shakes down an innocent business owner. The mafia says, "Give me 10 percent of your receipts or I'll burn down your store." The NCAA says to the student-athlete, "Give me all of your talent, for free, or I won't let you play." And like the mafia, the NCAA has its unbreakable rules. "Take money from a booster, cheat on an exam, go to a prep school diploma mill, or do anything else to embarrass us, and we'll take away your scholarship." If the schools break the NCAA's rules, they lose scholarships, are banned from lucrative postseason play, and have their ability to recruit severely restricted. In short, the NCAA says to them, "Toe the line or we'll drive you out of business."

Viewed in that harsh light, what's the difference between the way Tony Soprano conducts business in the back room at the Ba-Da-Bing Club and the way that business is done in the NCAA conference rooms in Indianapolis? The honest answer is: very little. The NCAA, in many ways, is nothing more than an old-fashioned protection racket. And it's making more money than the Gambinos and the Lucheses ever dreamed of.

Serious sports economists are a little kinder in their analysis of the NCAA. They don't refer to it as "the mob" or label it "a criminal enterprise." They have an academic term to describe the NCAA that implies its predatory behavior: it's called a cartel. And for the remainder of this chapter, that's how we'll refer to the NCAA.

In his June 2006 study "The Economics of College Sports: Cartel Behavior v. Amateurism," Cornell University sports economist Lawrence M. Kahn said, "Most economists who have studied the NCAA view it as a cartel that attempts to produce rents by restricting output and limiting payments for inputs such as player compensation."

Like the mob, The Cartel didn't become really interested in the economics of intercollegiate athletics until it became big business. And it didn't take an interest in the integrity of college sports until questions about this ethical matter threatened the business model.

Kahn's right, of course. As soon as college sports became big business, schools had ever-increasing incentives to recruit top athletes. When free tuition, room and board, and cake classes weren't enough of an inducement to bring Moose to the state university, schools actually started paying players under the table.

To discourage these payments, which were bad for business, The Cartel adopted the "Sanity Code" in 1948, which limited financial aid for athletes to tuition and fees, and required that aid not be given solely on the basis of athletic ability. Rather, schools had to also consider financial need.

It didn't take long for the schools—and The Cartel—to realize that by actually enforcing some sort of minimal academic standards and putting restrictions on scholarships, they were limiting their talent pool, which in turn limited their ability to make money. And, again, that's what it's all about.

The conferences were the first to realize the danger that the Sanity Code posed to the college athletics revenue stream. So in 1949, several southern conferences threatened to leave The Cartel. That would have been bad. One way The Cartel maintains its power is by eliminating the competition (or keeping any real competition from getting a foothold in its market). Understanding that defections would result in a loss of power, The Cartel quickly responded. In the early 1950s, it amended its rules and again allowed athletes to receive scholarships solely on the basis of their athletic ability.

"Perhaps more importantly," Kahn wrote, "the NCAA set up an enforcement mechanism empowered to punish schools that violated its rules."

In other words, revenues were threatened, so they had to rethink the Sanity Code. So The Cartel changed the rules, with one caveat: step out of line and we'll whack you. Sounds like Tony Soprano to me.

It turned out to be a pretty successful business model—one that served The Cartel well for decades. In 1950, The Cartel had 387 member institutions. By 2006, the figure had grown to 1,024.

In 1973, The Cartel went through what a legitimate business would call "a restructuring." It divided its business units into three separate divisions, largely based on revenue. The top earners for The Cartel were in Division

I, which today produces more revenue than Divisions II and III combined. The Cartel tweaked its revenue model again in the late 1990s and divided its best earners into Division I-A, I-AA, and I-AAA, again with size of operation and revenue the determining factors.

"This segmentation," Kahn said, "is viewed by some as an attempt by the larger schools to protect their rents from being lost to the smaller schools."

Indeed, to belong to Division I-A, a school must offer minimum numbers of men's and women's sports, as well as offer scholarships with a specific minimum and maximum payout. To be in Division I-A for football, the school must also meet certain minimum attendance requirements. All of this, of course, is designed to protect The Cartel's monopoly and maximize revenues.

"According to the cartel theory of the NCAA, the organization has restricted output, defeated rival groups, and enforced collusive restrictions on payments for factors of production, including player compensation, recruiting expenses, and assistant coaches' salaries," Kahn wrote. "In this view, these activities of the NCAA lead to the usual consumer and worker welfare losses associated with monopoly and monopsony. In addition, the exercise of monopsony power is said to cause a redistribution of wealth from revenue-producing athletes to coaches and athletes in non-revenue-producing sports. Since the revenue-producing athletes are disproportionately nonwhite and of lower family income than coaches or non-revenue-producing athletes, this is viewed by some as a regressive outcome relative to a competitive market."

THE AIAW AND THE NIT GET WHACKED

With its organization, rules, and punishments in place, the primary focus of The Cartel became eliminating the competition and discouraging anyone who was bold enough to try to cut into its territory. In the early 1970s, the Association of Intercollegiate Athletics for Women (AIAW) got a harsh lesson in what happens when you try to muscle in on one of The Cartel's businesses. The AIAW was founded in 1971 to advance women's collegiate athletics the way the NCAA did for men's sports. The organization mostly floundered during the 1970s, but started to gain some traction toward the end of the decade, helped along by Title IX, the federal mandate that stipulates that schools that receive federal funding must offer an equal number of men's and women's sports.

The Cartel had to do something about this. So in the early 1980s, The Cartel began scheduling women's championships in all sports. But most of its efforts were too directed toward pressuring broadcasters into airing the women's basketball tournament along with the men's March Madness. It also coincidentally scheduled the women's NCAA tourney to take place at the same time as the AIAW's finals. By 1982, the AIAW was gone.

Another example of The Cartel discouraging competition is the National Invitation Tournament (NIT), which, at one time, not only rivaled March Madness, but was considered the more prestigious of the two postseason college basketball tournaments.

In 1960, The Cartel implemented a rule that required member schools to give priority to the March Madness tournament. That move eventually relegated the NIT to second-class status.

Despite a long history of strict—and effective—enforcement by The Cartel, some schools and conferences still foolishly thought they could muscle in on one of The Cartel's businesses. In 2001, the Metropolitan Intercollegiate Basketball Association (MIBA), a league made up of smaller New York–area schools such as Fordham, St. Johns, and Wagner, filed an antitrust suit over the NCAA's rules regarding tournament play. After four years of painful and costly litigation, the MIBA cried uncle. In the settlement, the NCAA bought the rights to the NIT for $40 million and compensated the MIBA an additional $16 million in return for dropping the lawsuit. In other words, The Cartel bought off the NIT. You leave us alone, continue operating as the little enterprise that you are, and we'll look the other way. It was that simple.

A FEW SETBACKS

While The Cartel has been mostly successful in protecting its rackets, there have been setbacks. In 1995, a Federal District Court ruled that The Cartel illegally colluded to hold down the salaries of assistant coaches. The case stemmed from a 1991 Cartel ruling that set a maximum compensation level for certain assistant coaches. They were called "Restricted Earnings Coaches," and their salaries were capped at $12,000 during the academic year and $4,000 for summer camps.

Several antitrust suits against The Cartel resulted in the 1995 class-action suit. The court decided in favor of the coaches, and after a long appeals process The Cartel, which, again, operates behind the front that it's overseeing "amateur athletics," was ordered to pay $55 million, to be divided among about a thousand assistant coaches.

Perhaps the most devastating blow to The Cartel's monopoly power, as detailed in Chapter 5, came in the mid-1970s. Fed up with The Cartel's stranglehold on college football television rights, a number of member schools formed the College Football Association. In 1981, the CFA was on the verge of negotiating a separate television contract with NBC. The Cartel threatened to expel any school that signed the contract. While the schools had their own television contract for football, they would have lost out on the lucrative March Madness money.

Despite this risk, the conferences called The Cartel's bluff—and won. In 1984, two of The Cartel's business partners, the University of Oklahoma and the University of Georgia, used the one lever that's effective against The Cartel: the law. You see, The Cartel, like the Mafia, is all powerful when it's operating on the street. When the deals are being negotiated behind closed doors or in The Cartel's offices, The Cartel has all the power. The one place where it's weak—just like the mob—is in a courtroom.

The Supreme Court ultimately ruled that The Cartel's ironfisted control of television rights was a violation of U.S. antitrust law. Individual conferences and teams were now free to negotiate their own television broadcast deals and did. The most successful example of this newfound unfettered freedom, of course, is the University of Notre Dame, which has the most lucrative individual television broadcast contract in all of college athletics.

According to Kahn, an economist's view of the quantity and price of televised college football games before and after the 1984 Supreme Court decision "shows a sharp increase in quantity and an even sharper fall in price between 1983 and 1985, suggesting that before the Supreme Court decision, the NCAA indeed was using its monopoly power to restrict output and raise price. Ironically, it also appears that in 1983, the NCAA was operating in the inelastic portion of its demand curve, since over the next two years, price fell by about [75 percent], while quantity only rose by 50%. If this interpretation of the price and quantity changes is correct, then the NCAA wasn't even fully exploiting its monopoly power before 1984, perhaps fearing litigation or attempts by some schools to negotiate separately with television networks."

The next setback for The Cartel was the bowl games. Emboldened by the 1984 Supreme Court decision on television rights, the newly independent football conferences worked hand-in-hand with the Bowl Championship Series to create the new postseason bowl system. As I detailed in Chapter 3, today it is the bowl committees, not The Cartel, that get rich off of postseason bowl-game revenue. The Cartel only gets a measly $12,000 consulting fee from each of the bowl committees.

As imperfect as the BCS may be in determining a national champion, it took a lot of power—and money—away from The Cartel. Furthermore, as the debate continues over the BCS and whether or not it truly results in a consensus national champion, The Cartel would like nothing more than to have a postseason college football playoff system that it could control.

CONTROLLING COSTS

Of course, the most effective means by which The Cartel controls its industry and ensures maximum profits is by controlling the players themselves. It does this through its four-hundred-page rulebook, which stipulates where players can go to high school, what courses they can take, what entrance exams they must take, when and where they can practice, when and where they can talk to coaches, when and where their parents can talk to coaches, and, ultimately, where they go to school and how long they can play. The players, less than 2 percent of whom will ever make it to the NBA, follow these rules because if they don't The Cartel will cut them off from the surest path to the one thing for which they've worked their whole lives: a college scholarship and a potential pro career.

Once the players are in school, The Cartel controls when and where they play. For instance, a player who transfers to another school must sit out for a year. This was the case with disgraced Oklahoma quarterback Rhett Bomar, who transferred to Sam Houston State. But this rule has more far-reaching consequences.

"If a low revenue school recruits a player who turns out to be better than expected, the mobility barrier caused by this rule might prevent movement to a school where one's marginal revenue product would be higher," Kahn found.

What exactly is "marginal revenue product"? In short, it's the amount of money a school makes off of the average student-athlete. According to the most recent studies, the MRP of a draft-quality player ranges from about $263,000 for women's basketball to $495,000 for college football and $1.4 million for men's college basketball. Given the recent increases in both the college football and basketball television contracts—especially the rise of the BCS and the new $6.1 billion CBS contract for the rights to March Madness—these are certainly low estimates by today's standards.

Of course, the primary way in which The Cartel controls its labor costs is by stipulating that the players can't be paid. They are strictly limited to a scholarship and stipend, supplemented by up to $2,000 of earnings from a job during the school year.

"Since the cost of tuition, fees, room, board and incidentals comes to roughly $40,000 at private schools, it appears that compensation is far below MRP for these revenue-producing athletes," Kahn found. "Computations such as this are taken by some as evidence that the NCAA does indeed use its cartel power to exploit top athletes."

While Kahn is correct about the dollar value of tuition and room and board, he does point out that there are intangible factors that must be considered when calculating the true MRP of a college athlete.

"College athletes receive training and exposure that enhance their future earning power," Kahn said. "If the value of this indirect compensation is high enough, then it is possible that total compensation to players does indeed equal their MRP, and thus the NCAA may not have or exercise cartel power over the athletes."

In recent years, The Cartel's control over players has been undermined by the ability of players to leave school early and become professional athletes. This is somewhat limited by the NFL's rule that players must be out of high school for at least three years before they're eligible for the draft; for the NBA, the rule is nineteen years old and one year out of high school.

"Both the NBA's new rule and the NFL's rule on underclassmen make the supply of athletes to colleges less elastic and thus increase the potential for rent extraction," Kahn found. "If playing college sports were most players' best alternative use of time by a large margin, then these conditions would seem to approximately hold. But potential college basketball players may seek other employments, in effect making their labor supply curves more elastic than otherwise."

Kahn notes that as of the 2001–2 season, of the 366 American players in the NBA, 115 of them, or 31 percent, entered the NBA before their college classes would have graduated, and fourteen never went to college at all.

"These figures suggest that many top college or high school players may be at the margin between playing in college and trying to enter the NBA, whereas in previous times it was rare for players to enter the NBA early," Kahn said. "If the supply of top players does continue to become more elastic, the NCAA may find it surplus-maximizing to allow higher levels of compensation for athletes, as ordinary monopsony models would predict. This reasoning could explain why the NCAA now allows athletes to earn money in a job on campus, although the $2,000 limit on such earnings may be too small to noticeably affect the supply of athletes."

TARGETING THE MOST VULNERABLE

Then there's the issue of race that's roiling college athletics.

"Many of these athletes come from an inner-city culture where there are only three ways out," said Nathan Tublitz, a biology professor at the University of Oregon and president of Coalition on Intercollegiate Athletics, a student-faculty group looking to reform college athletics. "Drugs, music, and athletics."

He's absolutely right. I'll get into this more in the next chapter, but many of these kids have been told since they were seven or eight years old that they had "special talent" in football or basketball. Ever since, they've been coddled by a system that makes special exceptions for them. It gives them extra help with tutoring (or, in the worst cases, passes them without actually grading the test), special tests, special schedules, and special treatment. And although Kahn tries to look at college athletics in the black and white of economic statistics, it's hard not to notice the disparity between black and white on the football field, the basketball court, and in the classroom.

"The participants in the major revenue-producing sports of men's basketball and football are disproportionately African-American," Kahn noted. "For example, in the 1990s, while black students comprised only about 7% of undergraduates at Division I schools, 46% of football players and 60% of basketball players at these schools were black. One can view this imbalance in either of two ways. On the one hand, minority athletes are receiving a scholarship and an opportunity to go to college that might not have been there in the absence of college sports. On the other hand, given our results on monopsonistic exploitation, it is clear that these athletes are bearing the costs of allowing the NCAA to collude over athlete pay, at least assuming that college sports would retain their popularity even if the players were paid market salaries."

In other words, it's like the Three Card Monte scam that plays out on street corners every day. From a very young age, athletes are told to hold onto this dream of athletics. It will get them through high school and through college, and will ultimately result in a big-time professional sports contract. When they go back to their neighborhood in Bushwick or South Central Los Angeles, it'll be in a Bentley. But as Kahn and other economists can tell you, it's all a fairy tale. It's a false promise. That's because these kids are told of the opportunity and riches that can result from college athletics, but they're never told that less than 2 percent of them will ever make it to the NBA. As such, they are the most tragic victims of The Cartel's monopolistic practices.

Coaches of color don't make out much better. A recent study of college football coaches over the 1990–2000 period found that only 3.8 percent were black. And among Division I schools in the 2003–4 academic year, 58.2 percent of male basketball players and 44.3 percent of football players were

"Black, Non-Hispanic"; in contrast, Black, Non-Hispanic representation in all male sports was only 24.6 percent.

Some economists see conference expansion and realignment as an effort to counteract the strict control of The Cartel. The Pac-8 has become the Pac-10; the Big 8 has become the Big 12; the Big Ten has added an eleventh team; the Atlantic Coast Conference has grown from eight schools in 1978 to twelve today, and the Big East has grown from seven members in 1979 to sixteen today.

"Many conferences such as the Big 10 have added postseason conference basketball tournaments that take place before the NCAA championships," Kahn said. "These conference tournaments can be seen as a partial consequence of the 1984 Supreme Court decision. These tournaments may partially represent the kind of entry in which the monopoly rents of a presumed NCAA cartel are reduced. That is, the growth of these conference tournaments likely adds to the supply of games and may dilute some of the monopoly power the NCAA tournament enjoys."

A LOSING BUSINESS

If The Cartel is effective, what happens to the revenues it generates?

"Are they fully dissipated in coaches' salaries, facilities, etc.?" Kahn asked. "Are some of them shared with the rest of the university? Does intercollegiate athletics indirectly generate financial benefits for universities through alumni contributions, state appropriations or attraction of better students? A reasonable first step in analyzing the impact of college sports on the rest of the university is to ask whether on average the revenue-producing sports earn a profit and, if so, whether there are direct transfers to the university generally."

The short answer is "no." As I've stated in previous chapters, the vast majority of college athletic programs require a cash infusion from the university—either through student fees, or direct cash transfers—to remain in the black. According to Kahn, Division I-A athletic programs, which are the most lucrative, took in $29.4 million in revenue in 2003 and had $27.2 million in expenses.

"Included in this revenue figure is $2.8 million of transfers from the university to the athletic budget," he wrote. "Thus, before accounting for institutional support, the average Division I-A program lost $600,000. The other Divisions also each lost money, with losses averaging $3.5–$3.7 million per school in Divisions I-AA and I-AAA; $1.3–$1.6 million per Division II member, and $279,000 to $742,000 per institution in Division III."

Furthermore, Kahn shows that these losses are not anomalies, but are fairly typical.

"Between 1993 and 2003, the average profit in constant (2005) dollars for each of the Division I and II categories was negative in each case, except for 1999, during which the Division I-A schools broke even. Schools in Divisions I-AA, I-AAA, or Division II with football lost over $1 million on average in each year, while Division II schools without football lost at least $634,000 each year. Division I-A has shown the best profit results, with losses ranging from 0 to $936,000."

As previously discussed, the main reason these schools are in the red is because their revenues go to support other non-revenue sports, especially Title IX–mandated women's teams.

"In 2003, for Division I-A programs, men's sports made roughly an average $6.1 million profit per school, while women's sports lost about $3.6 million, including institutional support (there were also $300,000 of losses on non-gender specific athletic items)," Kahn said. "Football and men's basketball were by far the most lucrative sports, raising $12.97 million and $4.25 million in revenue per Division I-A school in 2003, respectively, or about 59% of total revenues, including institutional support. Moreover, these two sports together generated an average of $7.95 million profit per school in 2003. The only other men's or women's sport to show an average positive profit was men's ice hockey, which had a profit of $353,000 per school."

So what's the conclusion of all this?

"Big time sports programs appear to extract rents from revenue-producing athletes and spend them on facilities, coaches' salaries and nonrevenue sports," Kahn said. "On average, college sports drain revenue from the rest of the university. However, there is some evidence of positive indirect effects on public and private contributions; and for the bulk of schools, sports success appears to generate interest by a larger group of students than would otherwise be the case, allowing universities to expand and have a modestly stronger student body at the same time. In this consumer-oriented era even selective universities need to maintain their appeal to future applicants, many of whom are future alumni or future voters for state legislatures, and having successful sports programs may be a way to do this."

Some readers may think I've been overly harsh in my assessment of the NCAA. After all, I did compare the NCAA president to one of the most ruthless mob bosses ever portrayed on television. I don't have anything against the NCAA president personally, but in some ways I really do think the comparison is apropos.

But if you think I'm harsh on The Cartel, you should listen to Sonny Vaccaro. Since retiring from the shoe business and embarking on his personal self-redemption tour, he has been the biggest critic of The Cartel.

"I don't think the people at the NCAA are bad people," he told students at the Duke law school. "I think they're so closeted by the enormity of their institution that they're blind. The money is off the charts. The NCAA is bigger than U.S. Steel, or the Godfather. They receive all these benefits off the backs of kids."

While you may agree or disagree with Kahn's analysis and my analogies, what will ultimately bear us both out is how the NCAA responds to the current groundswell over its new set of academic standards for student-athletes.

A NEW CHALLENGE

The Graduation Success Rate measures how well a school is doing at graduating student-athletes over a rolling six-year period. The Academic Progress Rate is the companion statistic, and it is a snapshot of how well schools are doing in graduating athletes today. I'll look at these more in depth in Chapter 11, but all you need to know for now is that colleges and universities have had several years to adopt these new standards, understand what they consider and how they measure "success," and prepare for May 2008. That's when the penalties started kicking in. Schools that fail to meet the minimum standards set by the GSR and APR have started losing scholarships and the opportunity to participate in postseason play.

In December 2007, at the Street and Smith's *Sports Business Journal* Intercollegiate Athletics Forum, GSR and APR were topic A. And if the conversations there were any indication, GSR and APR could go the way of the Sanity Code. In short, schools and The Cartel are quickly learning that even requiring minimal academic performance appears to be too much for schools hell-bent on putting together football and basketball teams that consistently earn invitations to a BCS bowl or March Madness.

"I think the jury's still out on [GSR and APR]," said COIA's Nathan Tublitz in a January 2008 interview. "Last year, the NCAA talked about how 45 percent of basketball teams in D-I, 40 percent of football teams, and 35 percent of baseball teams were going to be penalized. They've backpedaled significantly from that. I think a lot of schools are asking for exemptions. What's unclear is if the NCAA will give them."

The problem, Tublitz said at the SBJ conference, is that the goals of athletics and academics are divergent.

"The values within the academic community are not being carried by the athletic community," he said. "The end result is that there are still a lot of students coming into the university who are unprepared academically. We're setting them up to fail."

Sonny Vaccaro thinks the GSR and APR are discriminatory.

"It they continue on this grade thing, they're going to cleanse the whole sport," he said of The Cartel. "Don't believe that the educational system in America is an equal opportunity system. These kids come from different backgrounds. They are bereft of getting a good education before they even try to go to a D-I school.

"I can't believe they sit up in their monument to themselves and make these rules without thinking of the opportunities for the kids who participate under these rules."

Vaccaro noted that during the NCAA Tournament, the participating schools run ads touting their academics.

"What they don't tell you is that because those kids are playing that basketball game, and they're getting six billion dollars from CBS, that's how they pay for it," he said. "They generated the money off these kids."

"I don't think kids should be paid," he said. "I want them to be treated like human beings."

The smart money says that when push comes to shove on GSR and APR, The Cartel will punt—again. And, as always, the one group that will be hurt the most will be the one group we really haven't talked about yet: the student-athletes.

11 THE KIDS

Go to any gym or ball field anywhere in America today, and you can plainly see the depth, breadth, and reach of college and professional athletics into our youth sports culture. Stop by The Oval in Roseville, Minnesota, and you'll see parents teaching their one-and-a-half-year-olds how to ice skate. This public ice-skating rink, one of hundreds in "the State of Hockey," has training aids that look like walkers. The kids, some of whom can't even walk yet, maintain an iron grip on the handles while their feet scissor back and forth wildly, trying to propel them along the ice. Eventually they get it, and before they're three years old they're skating like the pros they one day hope to be.

If they're any good, by the time they're six or seven they'll be on one of the elite traveling teams that hold tryouts to fill their rosters. These kids' moms and dads spend upward of $10,000 a year on equipment, fees, and private lessons, and countless hours on wooden bleachers in bone-chillingly cold ice arenas, watching the child that they hope will one day grow up to play in the Mariucci Arena for the University of Minnesota and, one day, maybe, the NHL.

In Southern California, the sport is baseball. Kids as young as seven and eight are playing baseball year round, going to elite camps, and hiring personal pitching coaches. By the time they're fourteen, dad will start talking to them about Tommy John surgery. Kids fourteen to seventeen make up one of the largest demographics of those having the reconstructive elbow surgery today. If Junior wants to make it into the Major Leagues, the argument goes, he'll have to have the surgery sooner or later; it might as well be now. Never mind that he's irreparably destroying the tendons and ligaments in his arm because he's pitching too hard, too fast, too young.

In Pennsylvania, Texas, and Florida, this youth sports mania infects Pop Warner football. By the time the kids are in third grade, overly obsessive parents are on league committees, manipulating the rosters to make sure that "the right kids" are on the right teams. By "right kids" they mean the biggest, fastest, and strongest. They want these kids to start playing together now in the hope that they'll build a level of teamwork and unit cohesiveness that will one day propel them to the state high school football championship and put their little burg on the map. To do that, they'll encourage their kids to start lifting weights and taking diet supplements, hire a personal strength and conditioning coach, and send the kids to elite football camps to get noticed by the college and pro scouts that prowl these camps every summer.

In tony suburbs across the country—Ridgewood, New Jersey; Walnut Hill, Ohio; Evanston, Illinois; and Agoura Hills, California—the sports that parents obsess about are golf, tennis, and, increasingly, lacrosse. The kids are holding a racket or club by the time they're three, while mommy gets a facial and daddy's on the back nine. These parents are too busy to be at every match. Dad's in Hong Kong, negotiating Asian film rights or the latest bailout package for struggling U.S. banks. Mom's finding her inner self at a Buddhist retreat center in Malibu, or at the doctor's office, shopping for a tummy tuck, liposuction, and a pair of 38Cs. These parents either drop their kids off at practice or have the French au pair do it. While they may appear more detached and attend fewer games, the flame burns no less intense. Deep down, they hope that their little Tiffany or Chad will become the next Jennifer Capriati or Tiger Woods.

What's often not discussed is the fact that less than 2 percent of these kids—regardless of which sport they choose—will ever have a meaningful pro career. Of the one hundred or so kids who show up to summer football camp at colleges across the country every year, less than 2 percent of them will be offered an NFL contract, and less than 1 percent will actually have an NFL career of more than a few years.

So why do they do it? Why do these student-athletes—pushed by their parents and coaches—think they'll make it to the pros? Because every one of these kids truly believes that they'll beat the odds. Each believes that he or she will be the one that makes it. And who can blame them? That's what they've been told since the day they could understand complex sentences or they first discovered that they had what they thought was "talent." The message has been drilled into their heads, over and over and over. Work hard. Play hard. And you, too, will be the next Derrick Rose or Tim Tebow. In reality, very few of them will even play on a Division I team. These kids—and that's what they are, nothing more than kids—are truly the saddest victims of the money-driven culture of college athletics.

I've purposely avoided saying too much about the players until now. I wanted readers to be well grounded in the economics of college athletics. I wanted you to have a clear understanding of just what a well-oiled multibillion-dollar moneymaking machine this is. And make no mistake about it, it's designed to do just one thing: print money.

THE FALSE PROMISE

While it doesn't take a rocket scientist to figure out what drives big-time college athletics today, this is the system that parents feed their kids into every day. They begin long before their kid is even close to stepping onto the playing field or hardwood floor of a successful Division I team. For some, it starts the minute they can hold a ball. It escalates into years of training. It means hours spent riding in cars, back and forth to practice, to elite summer camps, or as part of traveling squads that begin for kids as young as seven or eight. It may involve moving to the right city or state, to attend the right high school, to be close to the right coach, or to play on the AAU team that'll get you noticed by the scout who will whisper your name into the ear of the assistant athletic director for recruiting who will include your bio (along with a thousand other kids just like you) in a 2:00 A.M. slide show in the basement of a multimillion-dollar training facility and say, "We should take a look at this kid."

If you're one of these kids, your whole life has revolved around one sport. You've had coaches, tutors, strength and conditioning trainers, nutritionists, and dieticians poking and prodding you since you could lace up a pair of shoes. Most of your teachers have given you extra time to do your homework (or don't require you to do it at all). They make exceptions for your travel schedule and practices, and allow you to take tests whenever it's convenient for you. Most of your classmates don't have the courage to pierce the almost impenetrable bubble of celebrity that surrounds you. If they do, it's to offer nothing more than a pat on the back and an "Atta boy," something you've become all too used to hearing by the seventh or eighth grade. Others just smile and look away as you pass them in the hall, knowing that you inhabit a place in the universe that most of them will never know. When you're tired and want to quit, an army of coaches, guidance counselors, teachers, and trainers encourage you to "Hang in there." They tell you, "This is your ticket out." And your parents—especially your dad— reinforce it all. They scrimp, they save, they spend every last dime they have to make sure you have all the tools and training you need to make it.

If you're from Bushwick or Detroit or the South Side of Chicago or Watts or the wrong side of the tracks in any other big city or small town, it's likely your mom who encourages you to keep playing. That's because you don't see your dad much—if at all. Perhaps you don't even know who he is. And while your mom knows that your chances of making it to the pros are somewhere between slim and none, she also knows that basketball or football is what gets you up out of bed in the morning and out of the house. More important, she knows it's what makes you walk by the kids on the corner. The ones who are the lookouts and runners and bagmen for the local drug dealer. She knows that given the choices you have in your life, this long shot, this fairly tale that has one chance in a hundred of coming true, is your last best hope.

When you finally get to college, you continue to live in a world apart from the other students. You live in a special dorm, eat special meals, and have a different attendance policy for English Lit 110. You have a whole new set of coaches, guidance counselors, tutors, study partners, physical therapists, and nutritionists. They make sure you get up in the morning, go to practice, go to the weight room, go to the team meetings, and show up for your study sessions. When you can't make it to class because you're at a preseason tournament or the Final Four, they take notes for you and write down the homework assignments. They might even write that essay you haven't been able to get around to doing. As long as you show up to practice, stay out of trouble, and keep a C average, it's all free. Tuition, meals, room and board. You even get $200 a month spending money so you can take that cute girl who smiled at you in Freshman Composition to dinner and a movie (just be sure you're back in the dorm by curfew).

If you get hurt, you'll be treated by some of the best orthopedists, physical therapists, and athletic trainers in the country. Their number one goal will be to get you back in action, scoring points, and helping your team make it to postseason play. After all, that's where the big payday is.

But if it's a career-ending injury, or you flunk out, or your eligibility is up, it all comes to a screeching halt. No more dorm room with a lounge, a Wii, and all the best games. No more steak at the training table. No more tutoring. No more special exemptions for homework assignments and bio lab. It's all over. And that girl who smiled at you in Freshman Composition is dating the guy who came off the bench to take your starting spot.

In the end, you realize that it was never about you. It was about "the program." It was about what you brought to the program. How many yards you gained, how many three-pointers you made, and how many national championships you won. More important, it was about how many tickets and T-shirts you sold, how many alumni donations you encouraged, and how many sponsorships you brought into the arena. And when you were of no use to the program any more, you were all but forgotten.

This is the meat grinder that millions of parents willingly send their kids into every year. Why? They know the statistics. They know the odds. Furthermore, they know what it's all about. So why do they do it? Because they think their kid's "the one." He's the one who'll beat the odds, never get hurt, win the title, get the contract, and marry the coach's daughter or the Brazilian supermodel. He's the one that'll make it.

But in reality, all these kids are is the raw material for a system that chews them up and spits them out the other end. As Kansas State's Phil Hughes said back in Chapter 1, all they are is "the entertainment product."

It's a product that the system starts developing long before they get to high school. And no one ever tells them the truth until it's too late. A perfect example is Derrick Rose, the guy that every high school basketball player aspires to be.

Raised in Chicago, Rose was the number-one-ranked point guard while playing at Simeon Vocational High School. He spent his NBA-mandatory one year at Memphis, helping the team to the 2008 NCAA title game against Kansas. Now he's a starter for his hometown Chicago Bulls. It would be great if every aspiring athlete's story ended so well. Unfortunately, Derrick Rose is the rare exception. He's held up as the poster boy of all that's good about high school and college athletics, but few stories ever turn out like his.

Here's the more common truth: of all the kids who play high school basketball, about 3 percent receive a Division I scholarship. About 2 percent of those kids will have a meaningful NBA career. So what happens to the 97 percent who don't make it? These are the kids who, like Rose, have been ranked since they were nine, played on elite Amateur Athletic Union travel teams since they were eleven, and were passed along by well-meaning teachers.

Put simply, these kids get lost. They have outlived their usefulness for the machine that churns out kids for America's elite basketball, football, and hockey leagues. They are cast aside, with no meaningful education and no prospects for a college or a pro career. It's a pretty sad reality to wake up to at age eighteen. And, unfortunately, there are very few people who have any motivation to try to convince them that academics is as important as athletics. But there are some such folks out there; one of them is Cindy Harris.

ONE OF THE HONEST ONES

Cindy Harris is the associate athletic director for compliance at Illinois State University. Instead of trying to figure out how to get around the NCAA's new high school academic eligibility requirements, she's trying to use the new standards as a wake-up call to the principals, guidance counselors, coaches, parents, and students who have focused on athletics at the expense of academics.

As college athletics has grown in size and financial stature, so, too, has the scrutiny, both from the media and the NCAA. And there's a lot to scrutinize. In 2007, the NCAA Division I Manual, commonly known as "the blue book," was 440 pages long.

"It used to be 480 pages, but they made the font smaller," Harris said with a chuckle.

Why does it take so many pages to say, "Study hard," "Don't let a student tutor write your term paper," and "Don't take money from strangers"? Because the NCAA's reach now extends well into high school and even junior high. These ever-evolving academic standards and guidelines are explained in a rulebook that's often vague and labyrinthine in describing what athletes can and can't do long before they make their first recruiting visit to a college campus or sit down to take notes in freshman English.

"If an eighth-grader makes a half-court shot at halftime of an NBA game and wins free tickets to a game, he's technically ineligible to receive a Division I scholarship," Harris said. "The rules are that crazy."

The net result is mass confusion for students, parents, high school coaches, and guidance counselors. Sometimes, it's even confusing for university officials, whose full-time job it is to not only know but comprehend all 440 pages of the blue book.

"With all the rules the NCAA gives us, you have to be a Philly lawyer just to keep these kids on track," said E. J. Caffaro, BYU's director of student-athlete academics.

Nowhere is this truer than in the area of academic eligibility. Questions have risen tenfold in the past few years because of new NCAA eligibility standards that require high school graduates to complete sixteen "core" courses in NCAA-approved disciplines. Adding to the confusion is the growing number of international students who are being recruited to play Division I sports. The math and physics courses may be tougher in Germany and Israel, but if they don't fit into the NCAA's neat little compliance formula, it takes a legion of lawyers to get the kid a scholarship.

Cindy Harris is at the forefront of this battle of wills and wits between compliance officers and the NCAA. More important, she's decided to do something about it and develop an NCAA eligibility seminar for anyone who will listen.

The seminar is called "Got 16?" a reference to the NCAA's requirement that high school athletes complete sixteen core courses in order to be eligible for an athletic scholarship. When Harris first started putting on these seminars, she only gave them a couple of times a year, either on the ISU campus in Bloomington or at one of the local high schools. But as standards—and confusion—have risen, she's found herself to be in high demand. Now she and her small staff of graduate assistants spend much of their free time traveling the state of Illinois, explaining the rules and requirements to concerned students and parents, many of whom don't have the slightest idea what they're talking about.

"If you have a 4.0 GPA and an 85 on your ACT, you probably don't need to be here," she told an audience of about a hundred parents and guidance counselors at Glenwood High School in suburban Springfield on a snowy November night. "If you're somewhere in the middle or failing some classes and you need this information because you don't know what a core course is, then you need to stay. What I'm about to tell you very well could be the difference between accepting that D-I scholarship or going to junior college for two years to tune up your manuscript."

The first question she asks is "What's a core course?"

Only a few hands go up, so Harris explains that a core course is one of sixteen required courses that high school students must take to be academically eligible to play college sports. In short, athletes need four years of high school English; three years of high school math that's Algebra 1 or higher; two years of natural or physical science; one year of additional English, math, or science; two years of social studies; and four years of additional courses from the preceding list, a foreign language, religion, or philosophy.

Sounds simple, right? Well, one of the reasons the NCAA blue book is 440 pages long is the plethora of exemptions and special clauses, any one of which could derail an earnest student's eligibility. For instance:

Academically advanced students can start taking AP courses in eighth grade that count toward their high school core course total.

Computer science classes only count if they're given through the math or science department and carry one of those designations on the student's transcript. This is so athletes don't use cake courses such as Typing 101 or Understanding Windows toward meeting the core requirements.

AP and Honors courses are weighted differently. An "A" in an Honors course is worth five core points, instead of the usual four.

Test scores must be sent directly from the ACT or SAT testing agency to the NCAA Eligibility Center (formerly known as the NCAA Clearing-house).

The NCAA lets students use their best scores over multiple tests. So, for instance, if a student scores 400 math and 400 English on the SAT, retakes the test, and scores a 350 on math and a 425 on English, he or she can use the two higher scores—400 math and 425 English, to meet the 825 minimum requirement. It's the same for the various parts of the ACT. But don't worry about the writing portion of the ACT; that's not required.

"Don't do poorly on the ACT and then take the SAT," Harris tells her audiences. "Take another ACT because you can cherry pick your scores."

The NCAA also lets students pro-rate their test scores and GPA to get a median average. In other words, the 825 SAT and 2.0 GPA are just minimums—and fungible. A student with a 3.5 GPA can score lower on the standardized tests and still be eligible, and vice versa. There's a sliding-scale index at the NCAA eligibility Web site that explains it all, as well as an interactive form for the sixteen required core courses. Students can plug in their classes and see where they rank. Harris encourages students and parents to visit the site early, and often.

"Start in ninth grade, set definite goals for yourself, and track your progress," she says.

There also are provisions for kids who attend multiple high schools.

"We have a ton of this," Harris explains. "We have some kids in our incoming class that have been to three high schools."

This is to keep honest the kids who hopscotch from prep school to prep school, looking for the right coach and the right GPA. Regardless of how many schools a student attends, or how many core credits they're claiming from each, the NCAA needs to see transcripts from all three.

Hurricane Katrina added a new wrinkle to all this.

"There are cases from New Orleans where the high school doesn't exist anymore," Harris said. "It was destroyed by Katrina, along with the student-athlete's academic records."

The NCAA, she said, is addressing these on a case-by-case basis.

Student-athletes must complete all their core courses with the class they started high school with. In the United States it's four years. In Hungary, it's three. In Canada it's five.

"You have to graduate with your class," Harris said. "Finish everything. All tests. All written requirements. You have to walk across the stage and get your diploma."

Unless you're just one class shy of the magic sixteen. Then you can go to summer school.

Most important, students should make sure that the core course on their transcript exactly matches the core course on the NCAA Web site. If the guidance office makes a typo and sends in a transcript that lists an "A" in Calculus 3 instead of Calculus III, it won't count.

"If a course isn't on your high school's core list, it won't count either," she tells parents.

What's the point of all this?

"If you do well in the core courses, you will succeed in college," Harris said. "NCAA research bears this out. The better prepared you are, the more rigorous courses you take in high school, the better you are prepared for college."

That's the party line, anyway. The real reason is to support the NCAA's long-held façade—and that's being polite—that these kids are amateur athletes who are sociology majors first and basketball players second. As the money generated by college athletics has grown from millions to billions, and the recruiting and academic scandals have multiplied, it has been an increasingly difficult story line to sell. So the NCAA has tightened up academic standards to prop up its argument that these $100,000-scholarship athletes, playing in $100 million stadiums that generate broadcast rights in the billions are "amateurs."

Whatever the motivation, this new regimen of core courses and test scores is part of a bevy of much tougher academic standards put forth by the NCAA. And it's no longer enough that students' high school or state says they have successfully completed the academic requirements to graduate. The NCAA wants to check their work. That's why it created the Eligibility Center. The primary goal is to police high schools that allow star athletes to skate through on a curriculum filled with gym and soft social sciences, or the strip-mall diploma mills that masquerade as prep schools, where students spend more time working on their free throws than on Thoreau.

FOLLOWING THE MONEY

The NCAA also has modest checks on a student's amateur status, but it's mostly self-reported. Students not only must register with the Eligibility Center but must answer a series of questions:

Have you ever taken money from an agent?
Have you ever been paid to play?
Have you ever done a commercial?

Until they've done this, stepping foot on campus is a clear recruiting violation.

Never mind that the NBA only requires students to attend one year of college, or the NHL's new collective bargaining agreement allows teams to pay lower minimum salaries to first-year players, thus resulting in an exodus of top talent from big-time D-I programs like Minnesota and North Dakota. The net result is a whole new way of doing business for the NCAA, and a far cry from when Cindy Harris first started in this business.

Harris, now forty-seven, was a scholarship volleyball player from tiny Buffalo, Illinois. Her high school graduating class had fifty-two kids. Schools were the sole decision makers back in the 1980s, and ISU decided that she was academically eligible for a four-year volleyball scholarship. She majored in psychology and had a 3.8 GPA, but after four years wasn't sure what she wanted to do.

"I wasn't 'jockified,'" she said. "And I couldn't go play pro volleyball."

So she followed her college coach to Utah, became a grad assistant and got her Master's degree in sports psychology, and started coaching herself. Next came an assistant coaching position at Penn State and then her first stint as a compliance officer, at Valparaiso State University, about an hour southeast of Chicago.

"I knew next to nothing about compliance," she said. "Valparaiso must have assumed that if I was at Penn State, I followed the rules."

She started keeping recruiting logs and read the NCAA manual—a few times. One day, men's basketball coach Homer Drew came into her office and asked about recruiting kids from a foreign country. She had no idea.

"It was before the Clearinghouse, when schools made their own eligibility decisions."

That's where the trouble started.

"We would say a kid was eligible, and Wisconsin-Green Bay would say they weren't," she said. "It was that ad hoc."

This scattershot approach to eligibility—at a time when transcript doctoring was often the rule, not the exception—was what led the NCAA to create the Clearinghouse. But as with most government regulations, the tendency is to over-regulate rather than provide a sensible framework. This is how one or two smart guidelines evolve into a 440-page rule book that no one fully understands.

"What scares me is the things I can't control," Harris said.

Like boosters.

"I can't control a booster who approaches a player and gives them money," she said. "You can educate your boosters, but you can't control what they do."

Or summer jobs.

"When a student-athlete works somewhere during the summer, we tell our boosters that they can only pay them what they would pay someone else. And they can't get special treatment, such as extra days off."

And no matter how hard she tries, she knows small infractions are going to occur.

When Harris first started at Valparaiso, she had all she could do to meet the minimum requirements and went to bed every night praying that she hadn't missed something or that no athlete or booster would show up on the front page of the local paper the next morning. When she was given a graduate assistant to help her out, she started digging a little deeper.

"We started to pour over the phone logs, reporting more secondary violations."

Often it was just errors, or minor infractions.

"We discovered that a booster bought the little brother of one of our players a meal at a tailgate," she said. "We asked the parents to send us $7. We had to determine the value of the hot dog and bill them."

REALITY SETS IN TOO LATE

Where Harris has the toughest time getting through to kids is the inner city. I say "kids" because parents in these neighborhoods don't show up too much: parent-teacher conferences, school plays, or seminars about getting into college. I accompanied Harris to a seminar she gave at Marshall High School in inner-city Chicago in 2008. It was not only sobering, but sad. Over the hour-long presentation to about thirty students, all black and all poor, she laid out the new eligibility requirements. Around the room, the expressions on the young faces told the whole sad story. They had never heard of the NCAA Eligibility Center or the sixteen core courses. Worse, most knew that they were nowhere near where they needed to be academically. All hope drained from their faces.

When she finished, there weren't many questions. These kids were too devastated.

"What's the point of all this?" she asked, rhetorically, as she does routinely in these presentations. She continued, "If you do well in the core courses, you will succeed in college."

It was clear that these kids were numb as they quietly filed out. Only a few stopped to ask questions. No one had ever told them anything like this before. No one had ever told them that they have to be students first and athletes second. Many know they'll never make it.

So as happy as I am for Derrick Rose, I'm far more worried about the other 97 percent that we never read about in *Sports Illustrated* or see profiled on ESPN. Cindy Harris is a voice in the wilderness. Anyone who cares about the integrity of college athletics—and the academic mission of our colleges and universities—should join her cause. And those parents who we talked about at the start of this chapter, they should get on board too—to be sure that their kids aren't washed up at eighteen with tons of "athletic talent" but no future to speak of. Unfortunately, unlike North Carolina basketball or Penn State football, Cindy Harris is having a tough time recruiting and sticking to her program. That fact alone speaks volumes about how much universities—and our broader culture—care about academic integrity.

EPILOGUE

I wish I could end this book on a positive note, but I can't. To do so would be blatantly dishonest. The fact of the matter is that the issues of academic integrity, graduation rates, recruiting scandals, grade inflation, the facilities arms race, and the overall influence of big money on college campuses are not getting better, they're getting worse. Remember Derrick Rose from the last chapter, the kid from the inner city of Chicago who's a role model to every high school basketball player in the country? The one in 100 who "made it"? Well, turns out he didn't. According to the NCAA, in August 2009 Rose and the University of Memphis were under investigation for blatant recruiting violations. Allegedly, Rose had someone else take the SAT for him. As a result, Memphis was required to vacate its entire record for the 2008–9 season. As for anyone who proposes serious reform of this dysfunctional—some would say "criminal"—system known as NCAA athletics, they're merely spitting in the wind. That's because the simple truth is that money continues to trump academics when it comes to college athletics. A good example of the culture and corruption of big-time sports money can be seen in the 2008–9 college bowl season.

Players from Florida and Oklahoma, the two schools that played in the BCS National Championship game, received premium goody bags, akin to the ones they give out at the Oscars and at Fashion Week in Milan. It's one of the few times of the year when college athletes are allowed to accept gifts. And this year, Miami, host to the Orange Bowl and the BCS title game, was the place to be.

As described in Chapter 3, players in both bowl games were allowed to stroll through the Sony Suite, an exclusive room at their hotel stocked with Sony Electronics products. Each player had a $300 credit. Players picked out the items they wanted, including PlayStations and flat-screen TVs, and Sony shipped them wherever they wanted. Participating schools also typically order extra gift bags for big-donor alumni and other VIPs they bring to the games.

Players in the Orange Bowl and BCS Championship also received a Tourneau watch, Crocs, and an Ogio duffle bag. Players from the Champs Sports Bowl and Capital One Bowl, both in Orlando, were taken to a local Best Buy and given a $400 gift card. Other bowl gifts this year included Nintendo Wiis, Apple iPods, and Oakley Split Thump MP3 sunglasses.

Of course, sometimes these giveaways can backfire. Last year's Gaylord Hotels Music City Bowl in Nashville gave players a free year of Sirius Satellite Radio. Unfortunately, about twenty Florida State players didn't collect these goodies because they were caught cheating on a music test and weren't allowed to go to the bowl. Probably not the sort of publicity the sponsors were looking for.

Gift bags are just one example of how these bowl games, originally designed to promote tourism, have become multimillion-dollar enterprises in their own right. Revenues for the thirty-four postseason bowl games range from just over $1 million for the R&L Carriers New Orleans Bowl to more than $30 million for each of the five BCS games. College bowl games are an estimated $400-million-a-year industry, and more than twenty of the bowl games have tax-exempt status.

Yes, the college bowl games generate some pretty impressive financial numbers. But Derrick Jackson, a columnist for the *Boston Globe*, comes up with his own numbers each year: the bowl teams' graduation rates.

"Florida has a 68 percent graduation rate but a 25-percentage-point racial disparity," he wrote in his December 13, 2008, column. "Oklahoma should flat-out be disqualified with a 46 percent graduation rate."

Mr. Jackson also found that four other schools that played in BCS bowl games—Ohio State, Texas, Alabama, and Utah—all have black graduation rates under 50 percent and an average racial gap of 30 percentage points.

The NCAA has vowed to hold student-athletes to higher academic standards, but as Jackson points out in his annual column, graduation rates take a back seat to a winning record. In 2008 the NCAA instituted new Academic Progress Rate and Graduation Success Rate standards. But just six months after they took effect, there was already pressure to lower the standards. One person who's fighting to make them even tougher is Nathan Tublitz, a professor of neurobiology at the University of Oregon and co-chairman of the Coalition on Intercollegiate Athletics, a group of fifty-six Division I faculty senates whose primary mission is to remind college presidents, athletic directors, and coaches that these kids are supposed to be students first and athletes second.

It's a quaint notion in an era when CBS is paying $6.1 billion for the broadcast rights to March Madness. While Dr. Tublitz and his colleagues spend much of their time howling into the wind, it's fair to say that they are making progress, albeit limited.

The NCAA has long had its Graduation Success Rate (GSR), a six-year rolling average that measures how successful schools are at graduating athletes. And 2008 marked the fourth and final year of the gradual implementation of the new Academic Progress Rate (APR), a more real-time measure of an athletic department's academic progress. When the new APR numbers came out in May 2008, schools that fell short of the tougher standards were subject to increasingly harsher penalties, including lost scholarships and, if they prove to be chronic laggards, banishment from the postseason tournaments and bowl games that are their financial lifeblood. This was all good news for Dr. Tublitz and others who've long argued for serious academic reform of college athletics.

"The GSR and APR are, potentially, very effective tools to improve academic standards and to allow student-athletes to achieve their educational goals," Dr. Tublitz said in an interview. "The key, of course, is in the implementation and enforcement of penalties that follow from schools that don't meet the standards."

In short, Dr. Tublitz continues to be concerned that the APR—like many of the rules that govern recruiting, scholarships, and eligibility—will become for schools just another game of "catch us if you can." Furthermore, he worries that as the APR's true consequences are realized, schools will lobby the NCAA to water it down or make exceptions.

"In 2007, when the data came out and the trends were becoming clearer, the NCAA pointed out publicly that they were expecting 45 percent of basketball teams, 40 percent of football teams, and 35 percent of all teams in

Division 1 to be penalized under APR," Dr. Tublitz said. "The question is whether the NCAA will penalize all those teams that do not meet minimum APR benchmarks."

On average, Division I schools graduate about 77 percent of their athletes, according to the latest numbers from the NCAA. But the numbers run the gamut. For instance, in the Associated Press Top 25 for the week of March 10, 2008, number one North Carolina graduated 86 percent of its basketball players according to the NCAA's GSR measure, whereas number two Memphis graduated just 40 percent.

By the APR, the more real-time measure, North Carolina scored 993, well above the minimum requirement of 925, which the NCAA said translates into a 60 percent graduation rate. Memphis, by contrast, had an APR of just 916, which should result in penalties under the NCAA's new rules. As of this writing, none had been assessed.

Despite this, the NCAA insists that it's serious about enforcing the new standards, regardless of a team's national ranking.

"This is a real-time measure that has a component of accountability that's tied to consequences," said Kevin Lennon, the NCAA's vice president for membership services. "That's unique. We have not had this before."

Mr. Lennon also said that the new penalties will carry "a broader recognition" for teams that perform poorly in the classroom.

"We feel that under these new measures, they'll want to avoid being labeled as underperforming," he said. "And they want to avoid the penalties that will impact their ability to compete."

Dr. Tublitz concedes that there's only so much that the NCAA can do. The bigger problem is with a sports-mad American culture that doesn't care how college athletes are admitted, if they graduate, or if they ever make it to the NBA. All most fans care about, he says, is winning championships—whatever the cost.

"You have to stop the drift away from academics, and our universities are the standard-bearers for maintaining academic standards," Dr. Tublitz said. "Thus it seems appropriate for our universities to be the first in line to say we should reverse this cultural trend and not continue to look the other way when students are accepted primarily for their athletic prowess."

More important, schools aren't doing these kids any favors by admitting them when it's unlikely that they will succeed academically.

"We bring in seventeen-year-old kids, some of them from the inner city," Tublitz said. "We wine and dine them. They have female chaperones. We put them up in fancy hotels. They come here and see an incredibly fancy locker room with individual TV screens, air conditioning, and videogames. They go in and see the new football stadium and the new $200 million basketball arena. They see a medical training facility that is stunningly beautiful with waterfalls, treadmill pools, and state-of-the-art medical and dental equipment.

"They come here and are treated like royalty. Until they break a leg or get put on the second string and then they get set aside. Many don't earn a degree. They don't have the training or the skills to be independent after they leave the university. They're lost."

Indeed, as I've noted in previous chapters, only about 3 percent of high-school basketball players will get a Division 1 scholarship. And less than 2 percent of those who do will have a meaningful NBA career.

"What about the 97 percent?" Dr. Tublitz asks. "We need to give them the tools to succeed beyond athletics, and we're not doing that.

"There's a correlation between Oregon's attempt to have winning teams and the quality of students that they have to attract in order to achieve that goal," Dr. Tublitz said of his own campus. "This is not rocket science. It's not neuroscience. There are many extremely talented athletes for whom academics is not their primary goal at university. The fact that many people are OK with that says a lot about who we are and what we value."

Like Cindy Harris, Nathan Tublitz is a voice in the wilderness. He's broadcasting warnings about a very real threat to the academic integrity of our colleges and universities, but no one's listening. Furthermore, the influence of coaches who helm successful (that is, profitable) college athletics programs is growing to the point that they're candid about the academic exemptions that their players not only receive but apparently deserve. Case in point is South Carolina football coach Steve Spurrier, who was so upset when two of his promising young recruits were denied admission because they failed to meet NCAA academic standards that he threatened to quit.

"As long as I'm the coach here, we're going to take guys that qualify (under NCAA guidelines)," Spurrier said during a 2007 press conference. "If not, then I'll have to go somewhere else because I can't tell a young man, 'You come to school here,' he qualifies, and not do that. And we did that this year."

Wide receiver Michael Bowman of Wadesboro, North Carolina, and defensive back Arkee Smith of Jacksonville, Florida, who signed with South Carolina in February 2007, were both denied admission for failing to meet basic academic standards. Spurrier disagreed with the players being denied admission and went so far as to say that he was "embarrassed" that he and his coaches had "basically misled these young men into believing they were coming here."

Spurrier was so incensed by the incident that he spent the first four minutes of South Carolina's football media day complaining about the admission denials. Spurrier insisted he wasn't "blasting" the president or Provost Mark Becker. But he said he was speaking out to let high school coaches and players, as well as their parents, "know that that's not going to happen here if I continue to be the coach, and I plan on being the coach here a long time."

This wasn't the first time that Spurrier had fought with the administration to try and get his players admitted. In 2006, Spurrier said during the media conference that he "begged and pleaded" to have two players admitted, and the provost "relented." Both players, whom Spurrier didn't identify, started in 2006. In 2008, he pled on behalf of three players. One, whom he didn't identify, was admitted.

"We can have a heck of a big-time college football program here if we want to do things the right way, and we've got to do things the right way," Spurrier said.

"I truly believe this is the last year this is going to happen because I can't operate like that. I can't operate misleading young men, and our coaches can't."

Let me translate for you: in Steve Spurrier's world, if he wants two players to be on the South Carolina football squad, they're going to be on the squad. And nothing as silly as academic standards is going to keep them off campus.

Ole Miss found itself in a similarly embarrassing situation in 2007.

Jerrell Powe, a five-star defensive tackle from Waynesboro, Mississippi, originally signed with Ole Miss in 2005 but did not qualify academically. He then attended prep school at Hargrave Military Academy and signed again with the Rebels in 2006. The NCAA then questioned some correspondence courses he'd taken with BYU, saying he couldn't have completed the work without "significant assistance."

Powe's case was not helped when his mother was quoted in court papers as saying, "Jerrell is a really good child but he just can't read."

Powe's family filed suit to get a temporary injunction so that he could be admitted but eventually withdrew the action. The NCAA took the unique step of laying out an academic road map for Powe to gain initial eligibility: take some high school courses over again or attend junior college.

Powe elected to take the high school courses. Part of the process involved taking some courses online and attending a Spanish class in Jackson, Mississippi. Even after all that, the NCAA required a twenty-seven-point list of things it needed to see before ruling on the player.

In short, the NCAA system of college athletics is broken. It is financially and academically corrupt, and morally bankrupt. This systems drives more than "college ball." It affects our economy, our youth, and our society at large. Worst of all, it earns its profits off the free labor of kids, many of whom don't know how to read, write, or do basic math. Not only will they never graduate from college, 97 percent of them will never sign a professional sports contract.

And no one seems to care.

Not the coaches.

Not the college presidents.

Not the NCAA.

Not their parents.

Not society.

This is the sad state of the culture and economics of the NCAA. And even by the most generous assessment, it's only getting worse. As the money increases in college sports, there seems to be a direct and corresponding increase in our overall apathy.

Where does it end?

REFERENCES

Note: Unless otherwise indicated, direct quotations are from interviews conducted by the author.

Introduction

Shoop, Robert J. *A University Renaissance: Jon Wefald's Presidency at Kansas State*. Manhattan, KS: AG Press, 2001.

Wolverton, Brad. "Growth in Sports Gifts May Mean Fewer Academic Donations." *Chronicle of Higher Education*, October 5, 2007.

Chapter 1

Dohrman. "U Basketball Program Accused of Academic Fraud." *St. Paul Pioneer Press*, March 10, 1999, A1.

Chapter 2

The Carnegie Report, 1929.

Chaney, John. "Losing Proposition." *New York Times*, March 10, 1999, p. 19.

Dealy, Francis X. Jr. *Win at Any Cost: The Sell Out of College Athletics*. New York: Carol Publishing, 1990.

Lawrence, Paul R. *Unsportsmanlike Conduct: The National Collegiate Athletic Association and the Business of College Football*. New York: Praeger, 1987.

Sperber, Murray. *Onward to Victory*. New York: Henry Holt, 1998.

Stinson, Jeffrey L., and Howard, Dennis R. "Winning Does Matter." *Journal of Sports Management*, July 30, 2008.

Zimbalist, Andrew. *Unpaid Professionals: Commercialism and Conflict in Big-Time College Sports*. Princeton, NJ: Princeton University Press, 2001.

Chapter 3

Baade, Robert, and Sundberg, Jeffrey. "What Determines Alumni Generosity?" *Economics of Education Review,* 1996, 15(1), pp. 75–81.

Jackson, Derrick. "Graduating to a New Standard." *Boston Globe,* December 4, 2006.

Reid, Scott M. "College Football's Money Bowl." *Orange County Register,* December 25, 2007.

Smith, Michael. "The $400M Bowl Business." *Sports Business Journal* (Street & Smith), December 3, 2007, p. 1.

Sperber, Murray. *College Sports Inc.: The Athletic Department vs. the University.* New York: Henry Holt, 1990.

Chapter 4

Ourand, John. "CBS's NCAA Ad Rates Hit High." *Sports Business Journal* (Street & Smith), March 10, 2008.

Strasser, J. B. *Swoosh: The Unofficial Story of Nike and the Men Who Played There.* New York: Harcourt-Brace, 1991.

Chapter 5

Barron, David. "Houston Outlets Set Sights on High School Football." *Houston Chronicle,* August 27, 2007.

Duderstadt, James J. *Intercollegiate Athletics and the American University.* Ann Arbor, MI: University of Michigan Press, 2003.

Spanberg, Erik. "ACC Sets Standard for Tourney Revenue." *Sports Business Journal* (Street & Smith), February 18, 2008.

Zimbalist, Andrew. *Unpaid Professionals: Commercialism and Conflict in Big-Time College Sports.* Princeton, NJ: Princeton University Press, 2001.

Chapter 6

Bentubo, Jim. "Opening an Arena, the UVa Way." *Sports Business Journal* (Street & Smith), May 28, 2007.

Nocera, Joe. "SKYBOX U." *New York Times,* October 28, 2007.

Schultz, Marisa. "Athletes Are Pumping Up Adrian College Enrollment." *Detroit News,* April 23, 2007.

Staff. "Johns Hopkins University Boosts Funding Goal." *Baltimore Sun,* October 31, 2006.

Wolverton, Brad. "Growth in Sports Gifts May Mean Fewer Academic Donations." *Chronicle of Higher Education,* October 5, 2007.

Chapter 7

Maisel, Ivan. "The Right Stuff?" ESPN.com, November 26, 2007.

"Million-Dollar Coaches Move into Mainstream." *USA Today,* November 16, 2006.

Zimbalist, Andrew. *Unpaid Professionals: Commercialism and Conflict in Big-Time College Sports.* Princeton, NJ: Princeton University Press, 2001.

Chapter 8

Fish, Mike. "Just Do It!" ESPN.com, January 13, 2006.

Wolverton, Brad. "Growth in Sports Gifts May Mean Fewer Academic Donations." *Chronicle of Higher Education,* October 5, 2007.

Wolverton, Brad, "Sharp Growth in Athletics Fund Raising Leads to Decline in Academic Donations on Some Campuses." *Chronicle of Higher Education,* September 25, 2007, http://chronicle.com/daily/2007/09/2007092501n.htm.

Zimbalist, Andrew. *Unpaid Professionals: Commercialism and Conflict in Big-Time College Sports.* Princeton, NJ: Princeton University Press, 2001.

Chapter 9

Abouhalkah, Yael T. "KU's Bill Self Makes Millions, but What About Mario Chalmers?" *Kansas City Star,* April 10, 2008.

"IU Faces New Ground as Clean NCAA Track Record Now Tarnished." Editorial. *Terre Haute Tribune Star,* October 20, 2007.

Miller, Jeff. "The Camp Connection." *Dallas Morning News,* September 24, 2006.

"OU Transfer Hits 16-of-24 in Victory Over Angelo State." *Houston Chronicle,* August 31, 2008.

Robinson, Charles, and Cole, Jason. "Bush Evidence Mounts." *Yahoo! Sports,* January 10, 2008.

"Sampson's Sins Don't Fall into Catastrophic Category." Editorial. *Indianapolis Star,* October 23, 2007.

Tarkanian, Jerry. *Runnin' Rebel: Shark Tales of "Extra Benefits," Frank Sinatra, and Winning It All.* Champaign, IL: Sports Publishing LLC, 2005.

Yaeger, Don. *Tarnished Heisman: Did Reggie Bush Turn His Final College Season into a Six-Figure Job?* New York: Pocket, 2008.

Chapter 10

Kahn, Lawrence M. "The Economics of College Sports: Cartel Behavior v. Amateurism." *Journal of Economic Perspectives,* Winter 2007, 21(1).

Epilogue

Jackson, Derrick. "Some New Highs for Graduation Gap Bowl." *Boston Globe,* December 13, 2008.